40

An Illustrated
World History

J. M. Roberts was educated in Somerset and at Keble College, Oxford. From 1953 to 1979 he was a Fellow and Tutor in Modern History of Merton College, Oxford. During that time he paid several visits to the United States, and held visiting professorships at the Universities of South Carolina and Columbia. He edited the extremely successful partwork publication, Purnell's *History of the Twentieth Century*; and in 1976 brought out his one-volume *History of the World* to great acclaim. In 1979 he was appointed Vice-Chancellor of Southampton University.

An Illustrated
World History
5

Design: Arthur Lockwood
Illustration research: Diana Phillips
Text research: Nicola Sissons

J. M. Roberts
Making One World

Penguin Books

Introduction

In the lives of individuals and nations, dates are often good landmarks. 1066, when Norman William landed in Kent, will always be a milestone in English history, and to most Europeans 1914 or 1939 will always be landmarks because the great wars which began in those years turned their continent's history upside down. But world history is not like that. There are very few moments when we can actually pin down a great change and 1500 and 1800 (which are the limits of this volume) are only very rough markers. To the millions of human beings who were born, married, sick, or who died, were plunged into poverty or raised to wealth in those two years, they were, of course, very important and memorable, but, in the history of the world, all they can usefully do is to focus our attention on the three centuries falling between them.

What mattered most in those centuries was that European civilization stepped forward for the first time on to a world stage. That civilization was transformed, too, in ways which were to make it the dominant force in world history for the whole of the nineteenth and much of this century. Putting it at its simplest, everything important that has changed the world since 1500 can be traced back to European beginnings or influences. From the fifteenth century until very recent times – the last twenty or thirty years – Europeans and their descendants have had more impact on history than anybody else. No one expected this, and no one planned it. Most of those alive between 1500 and 1800 would not have known it was going to happen. But it is the central story of the last four books of this *History*.

Not that it would have been easy to see that at the time. It might then have looked as if other parts of the world were making the running. Charles V, the Holy Roman Emperor who ruled lands as far away as the Philippine islands and the Americas from his central realms in Spain, Italy, the Netherlands, Germany and Austria, abdicated in 1556, this was a decade before the death of the Turkish sultan Suleiman the Magnificent. It must have seemed for most of Suleiman's reign that his empire was stronger and more terrifying than the Christian empire, which was the greatest monarchy of the European world. Even at the end of the seventeenth century, when Louis XIV of France held at bay the armies of most of Europe, and built the greatest European palace of his age at Versailles, he could not match the work of the Chinese emperor K'ang-hsi, whose campaigns ranged as far as Tibet and Taiwan, and who rebuilt Peking.

Europeans and non-Europeans alike would have for a long time found it incredible that the future of humanity lay largely in Europe's hands. Yet it did. Of course the great traditions of civilization like Islam, Confucianism or Hinduism have deeply affected world history too in the last four or five centuries, but for the most part only as conservative forces; and most of the changes these civilizations have undergone can be traced back to Europe.

The world thus remade by Europeans was more populous, wealthier and more prone to faster change than before. It was also becoming one world, with an economic and political life more interconnected than ever before.

The changes which have brought this about lie at the end of a long road. Only a little of it had been travelled by the end of the eighteenth century, which is as far as this volume takes the story. Most of the world's surface was then still under the sway of non-European civilizations or barbarism. But even by 1800 the initiative in producing change had passed into the hands of Europeans.

Contents

Published by Penguin Books Ltd
Harmondsworth, Middlesex, England

Copyright © 1981 by J. M. Roberts

Design and illustration research by IKON
25 St Pancras Way, London NW1

First published 1981

ISBN 064.005 3

Printed in Great Britain by
Hazell Watson & Viney Limited, Aylesbury, Bucks

Title-page pictures: by 1500 people of different races and cultures were beginning to find out about and even occasionally to imitate one another's ways of life. But this was a slow process and for the next three centuries the world was still for most people one of very distinct and different civilizations. Left to right: an eighteenth-century clay model of a Dutch businessman, made in China; a Benin bronze of a lady of the court; the Moghul emperor, Babar; and a French noblewoman in the sixteenth century.

Mankind in 1500

No one in 1500 could have had a realistic mental picture of the human race. No doubt people everywhere knew in a vague sort of way that other people unlike themselves lived in various places a long way off. Even in Roman times black and brown men from Africa had been seen in Europe, and white (or pink, or sallow) Europeans had first reached China centuries before. But no Chinese travellers to the West seem to have got much farther than Persia. No European in 1500 (and probably no Asian) had seen an Australian bushman. The Eskimos of North America and Greenland then still lived in complete isolation, and the full variety of the peoples of Africa and the Americas was unimaginable.

Ideas of the physical shape of the world were equally incomplete. It was still not clear to Europeans in 1500 that what Columbus had bumped into a few years earlier on his way to Asia was a new continent. Even when that did become obvious (as it soon did), it was a long time before the sheer size of the Americas could be grasped. Australasia remained unknown and the vast spaces of the Pacific were to be almost unexplored for much longer still. As for Africa, though the Chinese knew as early as the fourteenth century that it pointed south and not east (as western geographers long thought) and though in the next century European navigators might have a shrewd idea of how to get round its tip, and coastal and

'If we could see ourselves as others see us' – both East and West have in the past had the most bizarre ideas about the appearance of natives of distant lands. Yet they were almost always assumed to have features similar to those of the artists' peoples.

oceanic routes from it to India and Indonesia were well travelled by Arab traders, almost nothing was known by anyone of what lay more than a very little way inland. Arab geographers had for centuries talked about sailing right round Africa, but it had not actually been tried. Many stories were told, but most of Africa was to remain unexplored until far into the nineteenth century.

What had been known for a long time was that in distant lands lay great centres of civilization and wealth – Rome, Constantinople, Baghdad, Delhi, Peking were some of the best known – and that these were the capitals of peoples who lived in strikingly different ways. Probably most people saw the world as a matter of 'us' and 'them'. To the educated Chinese, Europe was a place known only by the report of Arab or Turkish intermediaries (one of the Chinese maps of the fourteenth century has about a hundred European place-names on it which are phonetically recognizable) and all non-Chinese were barbarians; to most Europeans, non-Europeans (with very few exceptions) were either Jews or pagans.

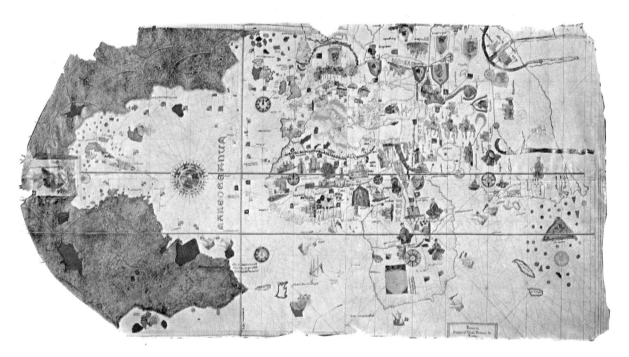

This map of the world was made in 1500 by Juan de la Cosa, who sailed on several voyages across the Atlantic with Columbus. Much of it is therefore based on the cartographer's own experience, but it is still wildly inaccurate in showing the world beyond Europe and North Africa. Yet only seventy years later a Flemish cartographer named Ortelius had enough information to be able to produce the reasonably accurate world map below, which was part of the first modern atlas.

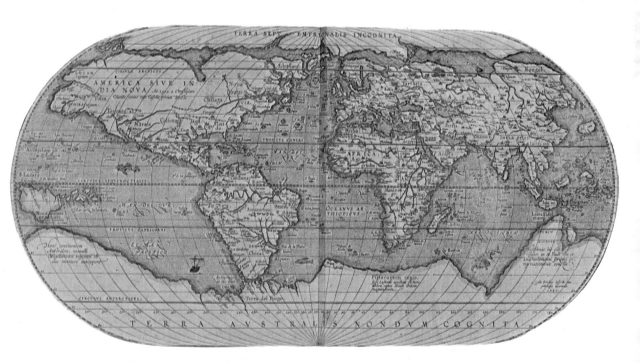

Other peoples took less exclusive views. But almost everyone would have sensed that in some places there were people with skins of different colours and different languages who were different in every other way too: customs, dress, ways of making a living, beliefs. They would not have spoken of 'civilizations', but they could, in a rather dim way, envisage the known world as a collection of them. Around each civilization still survived regions of barbarism, and few people from the civilized states had ever penetrated them.

This was much as things had long been. But in 1500 there were signs of change. More people had some idea of the world's enormous variety than ever before. Ships – which had been slowly improving in sailing ability and size for thousands of years – had gradually brought different regions more into touch by sea, whatever obstacles there were to travel by land, and one centre of civilization, Europe, had just begun to take more interest in the rest of the world than hitherto. Europeans had by 1500 discovered the Americas. There they were about to meet civilizations of whose existence, we can be reasonably sure, no non-American had until then ever been aware.

Yet, though geographical knowledge was rapidly improving, people in 1500 knew almost nothing about the structure and distribution of mankind, or its total numbers. In fact it is still very hard to make more than careful guesses about the way in which the world's population was then divided. Governments and scientists had not begun to collect statistics in a systematic way. Strong public feeling against taking a census persisted in Europe until the eighteenth century. For the most part, scholars have had to argue back from what they know to be true later, or to use such figures as they have for small localities (such as a parish with a good register) or special purposes (such as the medieval English Domesday Book). The results must be treated with much caution. There happens, for example, to be a fair amount known about population in Italy in 1500, but scholars still come up with estimates of a total which varies from five to ten millions.

Making the best of such information as we have, it looks as if the total world population in 1500 was about 425 millions, of which the largest part in any one continent was in Asia. The greatest single political unity in terms of numbers was (as it has always been ever since the end of the Roman empire) China, which can hardly have had much less than 100 million inhabitants. Probably the next biggest Asian country was India, though estimates of its population are very vague. Europe, including Russia, may have had eighty million inhabitants. After the enormous setback caused

Church registers are important data for population history, but other evidence can hint at overall trends, too. This brass from a church in Cornwall shows the seventeen sons and seven daughters of one sixteenth-century mother.

by the Black Death, when between a quarter and a third of Europe's population had died, the population in many places had not got back to levels of the early fourteenth century by 1500. In the sixteenth century France was the biggest single European country with something like sixteen million inhabitants, and was undergoing a burst of rapid growth. As for America, at the time of its discovery by Europeans, there must have been only about a million Indians and Eskimos in the whole of the vast spaces of North America – the largest single area still sheltering the old pre-agricultural way of life. Yet it looks as if there may well have been fourteen million Americans south of the Rio Grande in 1500, about five million of them in central Mexico alone, where a 'neolithic' life provided resources for more people.

In 1500 population growth was about to enter a new, unprecedented phase. Hitherto, slow increases had been followed by sudden setbacks. Though each wave of growth rose somewhat higher than the last, the overall rise had been very drawn-out. Time and again major setbacks had occurred. For years population would increase until there was no possibility of growing any more food with the land or skills then available. Then, one year, the harvest would fail, or a war or invasion would disrupt its collection. Starvation and disease would follow, sometimes very fiercely. The

onslaught of the Black Death had been like this. It came when a peak of population growth had been reached in Europe and many countries were over-populated. It killed so many farm-hands that food production fell lower still and it was a long time before enough was grown to support so large a population again.

We can now see, though, that populations in some European countries had already in 1500 begun to grow in an uninterrupted way which has continued to the present. What is more, though there were big differences between them (different countries grew at very different rates at different times), the rate was much faster than in earlier times. By 1800 this had begun to change the balance between continents. There then seem to have been about 900 million people in the world, about twice as many as three centuries before. This is not easy to explain, but the basic cause may be a spell of climatic improvements and better harvests. By 1800 more than a fifth of the world's population – about 185 millions – were Europeans, a larger proportion than ever before.

In 1798 an English clergyman, the Reverend Thomas Malthus, published (anonymously) a book which was known as the *Essay on Population*. It became the most famous book ever written about the subject and a great success. The book's popularity may show that people were again beginning to worry that there were too many people about and that the population was growing too fast. Malthus himself thought so and suggested that the outcome would be misery, as more people struggled for a limited amount of food. He tried to prove scientifically that this was bound to happen. Yet he wrote just when the rate of population increase was to accelerate faster than ever, and in a rising curve, but without every country running into tragic setbacks such as he thought inevitable. Changes already under way had made it possible to feed more people than ever before. These changes had altered the course of history.

A revolution in agriculture

For most of these three centuries there was a very broad similarity – as there had been throughout the history of civilized man – between what people ate in all parts of the world. It was nearly always bread or gruel made from grain – wheat, maize, rice and rye were some of many varieties used in different parts of the world – because growing grain is a more efficient way of getting calories out of a given area than raising stock on it. Unless circumstances are very special, it is a good rough rule that the richer a country is, the more meat is eaten there; all countries in 1500 were of course poor by modern European standards. Meat-eating had been more common in some European countries than elsewhere in the world even in the Middle Ages, but even in 1800 most Europeans rarely tasted meat. And, like the inhabi-

tants of other continents, they supplemented grains in hard times by chestnuts, beans and other vegetable foods. These hard times could recur in Europe even in the eighteenth century; there were famines in France and Central Europe in the 1770s and 1780s. Elsewhere, in China, Russia or India, and in parts of Africa, they have gone on down to the present day as appallingly as ever (though not usually with such prolonged effects as in former times, because food can now usually be brought quickly from some other part of the world).

In spite of all this, Europe differed fundamentally from elsewhere in 1800 because much more food was being grown there than three hundred years earlier. There had been plenty of room for improvement. Even a well-run and efficient medieval farm would seem a

Greece

Even today European landscape reflects patterns set centuries ago, when agricultural communities first discovered how to make use of the climates and soils at their disposal by farming in different ways and raising different crops.

England

poor sort of place to a modern European farmer. Given the amount of labour put into it, its output of crops was very low; seed corn usually yielded a crop only five times its own weight. Nothing like so much per hectare could be grown in 1500 as the same farm would grow today. Very little departure from traditional ways was possible, even if anyone could think of such a thing. In short, much medieval farming in Europe was like what still goes on in many parts of Asia and Africa today. Yet a change was coming and by 1800 it was irreversible. One result is that today more people than ever before have enough to eat. This is why the advance in European agriculture in these three hundred years is so interesting and important. It revolutionized human development more than anything since the invention of agriculture itself.

The Europeans had always had important advantages. Thanks to good rainfall much of Europe's land surface can be cultivated. Fish in the seas around the coasts provide plenty of easily harvested food. Under the earth lay important mineral deposits, including some of the richest iron and coal fields in the world. Before these could be properly tapped, there was abundant wood for fuel and building. Nonetheless, in 1500, most Europeans still lived as subsistence farmers – that is to say, they grew enough for their own needs, and only a few of them regularly produced a surplus to sell to those who did not live in the countryside. Even when they did, their market was usually very local. In spite of trade between countries in wine, wool, hides and a little grain, most daily food was grown and raised close by the place where it was consumed.

What was grown (and ways of growing it) varied a lot. For many centuries now a few big regional divisions in Europe have set the basic patterns of farming. One such is the division between north and south. Setting aside for a moment the Scandinavian peninsula, Europe

France

Finland

basically consists of two zones: a broad plain and a corresponding stretch of high, often mountainous country to the south of it.

With almost no disturbance except a slight rise to the west of Moscow, the great European plain rolls westwards for more than 5000 kilometres almost uninterrupted by high hills. It begins with the broad expanses of Russia, starts to narrow somewhat south of the Baltic, in Poland and eastern Germany, and then fans out again round the Ardennes and French Massif Central to taper away to the Pyrenees. Across the North Sea, England is part of it too, and it peters out in the foothills of Wales and Scotland. This expanse is Europe's historic grain-growing area. Grain has long provided Europeans with both food and drink. Beer made from barley, and spirits distilled from grains – whisky, vodka or gin, for example – are the traditional alcoholic drinks of this region. It has well-defined boundaries. In Russia there is the line of the northern coniferous forest. The sea provides a northern limit farther west and the southern flank is protected by the mountain-wall of the Carpathians, Alps, Massif Central and Pyrenees.

South of these mountains the ground is generally high-lying except for a few river-valleys,

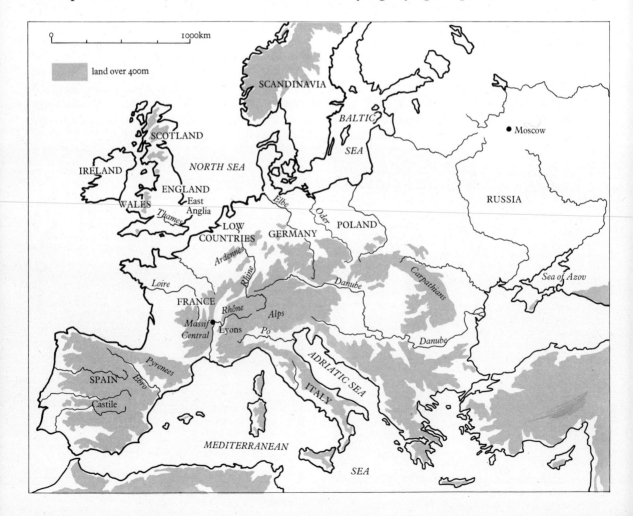

of which the Danube, Rhône, Po and Ebro are the most notable and important. Grain is also grown in this southern area in some places (the Danube valley is one, the plateau of Castile another), but the high ground is often farmed by stock-raising and pasturing. It is the land of the vine: wine and grape spirits provide its alcoholic drinks. Finally, around the Mediterranean coasts and over much of Spain, it is the land of olives, which provide oil.

Now look at the agricultural map again with a different division in mind. The Elbe is not a bad marker of the northern plain's separation into east and west. History has frequently taken different roads either side of a line from the mouth of the Elbe to the head of the Adriatic. Roughly speaking the same line runs along the January 'isotherm' of 0° Centigrade – the line which links places having zero temperature in that month. The west, warmed by the air and water currents we call the 'Gulf Stream', is warmer than the east, swept by belts of cold air from the Arctic and the land-mass of Asia. The Sea of Azov, for example, lies as far south as the French city of Lyons, but is often frozen in winter, while the Rhône at Lyons continues to flow. This division has had big consequences for east and west Europeans and the way in which they get their living.

One consequence was that they raised different crops. In eastern Europe until very recent times the hardy rye was the usual grain for human consumption, while wheat or maize (the 'Indian corn' introduced from America in the sixteenth century) were commoner farther west. Another striking difference was that (broadly speaking and with many local variations) most peasants west of the Elbe in 1800 were either freemen owning their own little plots of land or tenants paying rent in cash or kind, even if they had certain obligations to the lord of the manor. In the east they were much more likely even at that late date to be serfs, 'tied' to the soil of the manor on which they lived, unable to leave without permission. This difference became much more marked after the seventeenth century, when serfdom entrenched itself more deeply still in the east just as it was dying in the west. Many political and social repercussions followed from this.

Both in east and west Europe many more specific local differences sprang from the needs of husbandry in particular areas: soil, climate, knowledge and local markets all give variety to the picture. They gradually led to specialization, which had other far-ranging effects. Even in the sixteenth century, for example, grain grown in the lands south of the Baltic was shipped to western Europe, and this meant growth in the shipping industry and new profits for the old German towns of the league of sea-ports called the 'Hansa'. In fifteenth-century England East Anglia had already specialized in barley-growing and sheep-raising, while the Thames valley produced wheat, and the northern and western counties grazed cattle. Even the appearance and special qualities of animals were different in different places. The Merino sheep was suited to the dry pastures of Spain; it looked somewhat goat-like to English eyes, but it gave the best wool. (It was later to spread worldwide as breeders sought to produce more and better wool for new textile customers.) Sheep raised on England's greener pastures, on the other hand, had coarser fleeces but carried more meat. Many such variations meant that levels of well-being and comfort differed a lot from country to country. Foreigners noticed that peasants and craftsmen in seventeenth-century England wore woollen cloth, whereas their continental equivalents long wore coarse linens made from flax.

It would be easy to go on listing such differences, for there were many, but though interesting it would not do more than confirm the basic point: backward by modern standards as European agriculture may seem to have been in 1500, it was already pretty diversified. What is more (since nothing happens

A corn-harvesting scene in Flanders, detail from a painting by Breughel the Elder in 1565.

neatly in history), some of its variety was then already reflecting the first beginnings of the big transformation that was coming, the 'Agricultural Revolution', as it used to be called. Eighteenth-century Englishmen preferred the word 'Improvement', which is in some ways better than 'revolution', for although there was a change which, because it transformed the world, was indeed revolutionary, it came about only gradually and slowly, as people learnt what the new farming was and spread knowledge of it about. Why it should have happened in Europe is still much of a mystery. The basic explanation may be the slow accumulation of wealth and resources – particularly shown in the growth of towns – going on there since the twelfth century. But it is odd that something similar did not happen in, say, China, where a great growth of cities also occurred and where intensive labour and manuring (contracts for removing human waste – 'nightsoil' as it was called – from towns were very valuable in both China and medieval Europe) were employed.

Improvement took different forms in different places, but almost always meant specialization. Individual farmers stopped trying to grow everything and concentrated on the things they could do best, buying their other needs elsewhere. It was also always accom-

panied by technical betterment. This might mean new 'rotations' (that is, using fields for different crops each year in such a way as to rest and improve the soil rather than exhaust it), new products (potatoes and maize from America were outstanding examples), new treatments (liming, for example, for the soil), new varieties of familiar crops (special grasses for pasture), new care for the soil (building drains and hedges), new machinery (though this came in more slowly), or simply the enclosing of land which was formerly 'common' so as to make it the property (and therefore the interest) of one man. In the end, though, all these things led to more being extracted from the land, and greater production meant more food and cheaper clothes.

Some of these changes first appeared in parts of Italy and in Flanders in the fourteenth and fifteenth century. They were pushed farthest in the Low Countries, from which they spread to England in the sixteenth and seventeenth centuries. Some of the first results there were the enclosing of land for sheep, the bringing-together of the scattered medieval strips of an individual holding into compact fields, the draining of land (especially in the

Fens), and the making of new land from marsh and sea (as the Dutch had done). This laid the foundations for a tremendous technical advance in English farming in the eighteenth century, when it became the best in the world. New breeds of animal and varieties of crops multiplied, and the first important innovations in machinery since the coming of the wheeled plough were made in the shape of mechanical drills, horse-drawn harrows and threshing-machines.

In the eighteenth century people came from all over Europe to see English farming. The new methods spread back to the continent, especially to Germany and the east. Here, where the soil was often poor, it was doubly important to take advantage of every possible way of improving it. This led, paradoxically, to landlords hanging on even more firmly to something of the past. Since what was needed above all in eastern Europe to improve productivity was labour, landlords resisted all attempts to break up the old manorial system. Serfdom had virtually been replaced by wage-labour in England by 1500, but in the next two hundred years it became much more common in Germany and Poland (to say nothing of Russia). The *Junkers* of East Prussia, as the German noblemen were called, got as much work as possible out of their serfs, tying them more firmly by legal rules to the manor so that they could do so. In 1800 it was still quite normal for a peasant on an east German estate not to be able to leave it for a job elsewhere or to marry without permission, or to attend to his own patch of garden before he had done the

The calendar illustration (left) for the year 1529 shows seeds being sown by hand – 'broadcast' – with the old plough and rake in use in the background. By 1745 this sophisticated four-wheel drill plough, incorporating a seed and manure hopper (right), had been invented.

work he owed his landlord. (Nor was this work always due in the field; the serf's children and womenfolk might have to work in the house for the lord, too.) In Russia things were even worse – and were to get worse still – though technical improvement there was slight. Certainly improvement was far from being the only reason why serfdom persisted in eastern Europe while disappearing in the west, but it is part of the explanation. It was very convenient to tighten up the demands made on serfs if you wanted to improve your estate. In some places (Poland was one of the worst) the outcome was that peasants were reduced to near-slavery.

General progress often makes many individuals miserable. Still, it is hard to argue that the overall and long-term effects of improvement were not good. By 1800 there were still many hungry people in Europe, but in some countries they were far fewer than three centuries before; a corner in history was being turned by the Agricultural Revolution. And every side of life was touched by this because agriculture was the mainspring of the economy. Apart from minerals and fish-products, most manufactures and commerce depended on and dealt in things grown or raised on the land – hides for shoes, wool for cloth, grapes and hops for wine and brewing.

Europe in 1500

Since so many currents of world history swirled outwards from Europe between 1500 and 1800 it is sensible to try to see what 'Europe' meant at the start of this era. The area on the map now given that name looked very different in 1500 in everything except its outline. The simplest map we could draw of it then would have to show its religious structure, for Europe outside the area of Turkish domination was almost entirely Christian. Well to the east, Christendom was divided by the line at which Roman Catholicism gave way to Orthodox Christianity; there were borderlands in Hungary, the Ukraine and what is now Yugoslavia, where these denominations were rather mixed up. Roman Catholic bishoprics could be found as far east as Vilna and the Dniester. As for the Christian Europeans under Moslem Turkish rule, they usually belonged to one of the Orthodox Churches. In the next few centuries Islam was to advance still farther in Europe, by conversions among the Balkan peoples, but by way of balancing this the many Moslems who still lived under Spanish rule in 1500 disappeared. At that date there were also Jews in almost every European country, though some communities were very small. Most were to be found in the borderlands of Poland and Russia, to which many Jews had fled from persecution in western Europe during the Middle Ages. This would be the only big area where such settlement was important enough to require to be specially marked on a map. For the most part, geographical Europe was nearer to being the same thing as what was called 'Christendom' – the part of the world lived in only by Christians – than ever.

By contrast the political and legal map of 1500 was a terrible jumble. Spain, Portugal, England and France, it is true, looked somewhat like their modern equivalents. Each of them, of course, had good natural boundaries. The Pyrenees, the Atlantic and the Mediterranean cut off the Iberian peninsula; once the Moors were defeated, it was not easy for outsiders to interfere there. But Portugal had its own king, and Spain, though united under the same rulers, was legally divided into the kingdoms of Castile and Aragon, each of which had separate laws and customs. Up in the north too there was the little independent kingdom of Navarre. As for England, she was almost an island and her kings had conquered Wales long before. Yet she still had an independent neighbour in Scotland; though the two kingdoms shared a king after 1603, they were not brought together into one state, 'Great Britain', until 1707. Even then, many of their laws remained different. Ireland, though an island, was a conquered province ruled by an English viceroy until the eighteenth century. At that time English kings still called themselves kings of France; this was by then pure boasting or antiquarianism, but in 1500 England still held a tiny patch of land around Calais, though the French kings were effectively the rulers of most of modern France. Some eastern areas, notably much of Burgundy, Savoy, Alsace and Lorraine, had not yet been brought under their rule, though, and right inside France little islands of territory ('enclaves', as they are called) belonged to foreign rulers; the most notable of them was Avignon, belonging to the pope of Rome.

Most rulers had claims on lands elsewhere through marriage or descent. If there was one principle on which what we would now call 'international affairs' (the phrase did not exist then) was based, it was that family ties were all-important. The relations of European rulers with one another in 1500 were still shaped above all (as they had been for centuries) by the struggles of families to extend, strengthen and safeguard their inheritances. Broadly speaking, most statesmen thought of Europe as a patchwork of personal and family estates; pieces of land belonged to individual rulers and therefore to one or another of the major royal dynasties, just as different farms or houses in different parts of the same country might have the same owner. 'Dynasticism', as it is sometimes called, was the pursuit of the interests of a ruling family, rather than that of the inhabitants of a particular place. It was what Europe's politics were mainly about.

Two or three families were especially im-

portant. The Welsh Tudors had recently given a king for the English throne, but England was not a very powerful country in 1500. Though the Tudor Henry VIII did make a bid to become Holy Roman Emperor a few years later, English monarchs did not usually count for much in the sixteenth century except when other people were quarrelling among themselves and wanted their help or neutrality. The French Valois were more important. They had ruled France since the fourteenth century and had driven the English out after a long struggle; they cut much grander figures than the Tudors and lasted until 1589, when an-

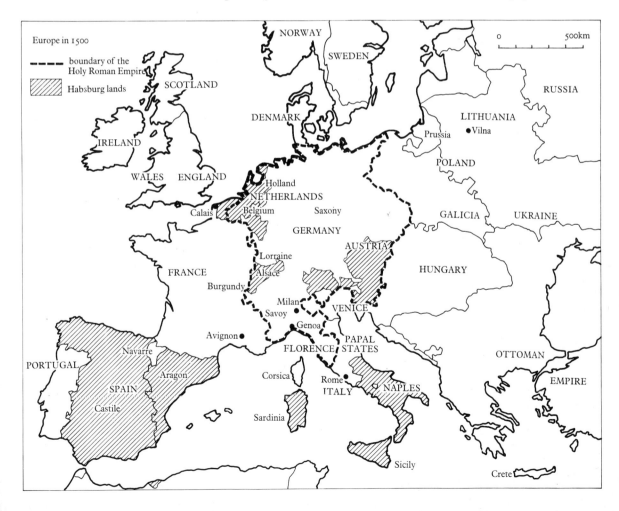

Europe in 1500

- - - - boundary of the Holy Roman Empire

▨ Habsburg lands

other highly successful line (related by marriage), the Bourbons, took the French throne. In 1500, though, both Valois and Tudor were outshone and were indeed going to be long outlasted by another family, the Austrian Habsburgs.

The ups and downs of the Habsburgs were to make up a lot of the story of European politics right down to 1918, when the last of them was driven into exile. The family had by then been ruling Austria for about six hundred years. Their greatest age began in 1438 when one of them became ruler of what became known about that time as the 'Holy Roman Empire of the German Nation'. Usually it was simply called the Holy Roman Empire or even just the 'Empire' and it was the remote but direct descendant of Charlemagne's empire. Much of it lay outside Germany, but it was there that the princes who elected the emperor were to be found. From 1438 until the Holy Roman Empire disappeared (in 1806, though the *Austrian* empire went on, and so the Habsburgs went on using the title of 'emperor'), the Habsburgs held the position of Holy Roman Emperor with only one brief interruption. In 1500 the second Habsburg emperor, Maximilian, was head of the family. His first wife was the daughter of one of the richest medieval rulers, the duke of Burgundy, who had no son to succeed him. The duke's death therefore caused a lot of trouble, and further complicated the map, for fragments of his inheritance passed into many different hands. But before this there was much quarrelling and trouble. One can view many events of the sixteenth century as a long duel between Valois and Habsburg over the Burgundian inheritance, notably its rich Netherlands provinces (roughly, modern Belgium and Holland). When, in 1519, a Habsburg who was already king of Spain became Holy Roman Emperor and united to the old Habsburg lands the empire of Spain, it seemed that the family might well be on the way to a universal monarchy. This was Charles V.

Habsburg and Valois joined other families in quarrelling about Italy, where they sought allies and satellites among the dozen or so major states into which the peninsula was divided. Some of these were aristocratic republics (Venice was the most famous and still had great overseas possessions in Cyprus, Crete and the islands of the Aegean), some virtually monarchies, whether they admitted it or not (like Florence, nominally a republic but really in the hands of a family of former bankers, the Medici). But these were not the only complications in Italy. Most Italian states fell within the Holy Roman Empire, but some did not, among them three very important ones – Venice, the kingdom of Naples and the Papal States, the lands ruled by the pope as a prince like any other prince.

Complicated as this sounds, the map of Italy is simplicity itself by comparison with that of Germany and central Europe. Germany was the heartland of the Holy Roman Empire.

1 *The Habsburg emperor, Charles V*
2 *A member of the rival Valois family, Francis I*
3 *His brother-in-law, who became France's first Bourbon ruler, Henry IV.*

1

2

3

During the sixteenth and seventeenth centuries the Habsburgs made great efforts to turn the empire into a centralized monarchical state, but they never succeeded. The constitution of the empire was chaos. It was supposed to provide the machinery for harmoniously running the affairs of about four hundred different states, statelets and notables. There were, for example, princes who were the feudal vassals of the emperor (among them the most important were the seven who elected him); dozens of independent imperial cities; the Habsburg family lands in Austria themselves; the fifty princes of the Church who ruled in their lands like lay sovereigns; the hundreds of minor noblemen – the imperial knights – subject only to the emperor as feudal dependents; the Bohemian and Silesian lands which actually belonged to the crown of Hungary (itself out-

The marriage in 1533 between the fourteen-year-old Catherine de Medici and Henry, Duke of Orléans, who later became Henry II of France. Although not of royal descent, the bride's family were extremely wealthy and ruled the republic of Florence. Though her husband Henry II died, Catherine, as queen-mother, lived to see no fewer than three of her sons ascend the French throne.

side the empire) and so on and on. This was a terrible mess, though taken for granted as a proper state of affairs. As Charles V had to govern Spain and its huge possessions outside Europe as well, the chance of exercising real control was virtually non-existent.

Not that stronger imperial government would have been likely by itself to have made much more sense of the map of eastern Europe. Not even all of Germany fell within the empire. Some Germans lived beyond it in the east, in royal Prussia, for example. On the Baltic coast Germans were mixed up with Swedes and Poles. Across the sea Sweden was an independent kingdom (including what is now Finland); Denmark and Norway shared another ruler. On the mainland again, the great sprawling kingdom of Lithuania covered much of modern Poland, Galicia and the Ukraine. Russia, farthest east, was expanding, but was then still little more than the northern half of what is now that country west of the Urals, and its Tsar was barely to be regarded as part of the European community of rulers at all. Finally, in central Europe another large and independent Christian kingdom, Hungary, lay between the empire and the Ottomans in the Danube valley, with part of its lands inside the imperial boundary, part outside.

A demographic map would be simpler than this and would show pretty well-defined regions. On or near the Mediterranean coasts lived perhaps half the continent's population in 1500, many of them in the oldest-established European cities. The first manufacturing districts had been the textile towns of central and northern Italy; these urban concentrations still had few rivals in 1500, tiny though many of their great cities would now seem. One other major urban region flourished in Flanders and Artois where, as in Italy earlier on, cloth-working had built up a more closely packed population than elsewhere. The Rhineland and old Lotharingia was another area where towns were common.

The European religious revolution

Early in the sixteenth century there came a great upheaval in European history, later called the Protestant Reformation. It marked the end of an era of European civilization and was to be of outstanding importance in world history. Yet, like so many great changes, few could have foreseen the Reformation and those who launched it would have been horrified had they been able to glimpse the final outcome of what they were doing. They broke a tradition of respect for religious authority going back a thousand years. They ended the unity of Christendom which they deeply believed in. They created new political conflicts though they often thought they were concerned only with unworldly matters. Looking back, we can see too that they were taking the first and most important steps towards greater individual freedom of conduct, more tolerance of different opinions and much more separation between the secular and religious sides of life. All these things would have appalled them. In short, they launched much of modern history.

In theory, Europe was still wholly Christian in 1500. So it had been since the Dark Age conversions of the barbarians. Only in Spain did Christian kings rule any large number of non-Christian subjects; the few Jews in other countries lived apart from Christians, segregated in their ghettos, taxed, but not usually enjoying the same legal protection as Christians. Apart from these special cases, all Europeans were Christians: the words almost mean the same thing in the Middle Ages. Religion was the one Europe-wide tie between men, and Christendom was an undivided whole, held together by a common faith and the work of the Church. It was Europe's only continent-wide legal institution. Church law operated in every land through courts alongside and separate from the lay system. Beyond the realm of law, all universities were governed and directed by churchmen. Finally, in every country the same sacraments were administered and imposed the same pattern on the great events of people's lives – birth, marriage and death.

In spite of its unrivalled position, there was plenty of criticism of the Church to be heard in the early sixteenth century. There was nothing new about this. Evils denounced in the Middle Ages were still worrying critics hundreds of years later – the ignorance of clergymen, for example, or their misuse of power for personal gain, or their involvement in worldly life. Many such ills – and others – had long been attacked, often by clergymen themselves, and great writers like Chaucer and Boccaccio had long ago poked plenty of fun at priests who liked drinking and chasing girls more than attending to their spiritual duties, and contrasted poor clergy devoted to their flock with their rich, self-indulgent superiors. Yet anticlericalism – that is, attacking the clergy – did not mean that people wished to forsake the Church itself or doubted the truth of Christianity.

Some clergy had tried to put their house in order. As the fifteenth century went on, some critics – many priests among them – began to suggest that it might be necessary to turn back to the Bible for guidance about the way to live a Christian life, since so many of the clergy were obviously not making a very good job of it. They were often labelled 'heretics' – that is, followers of erroneous and dangerous doctrines – and the Church had powerful arms to deal with heresy. Some of these men, the Oxford scholar Wyclif or the Czech John Hus (who was burnt), for example, had strong popular support, and appealed to the patriotic feelings of fellow-countrymen who felt that

By 1500 the Catholic Church had moved a long way from its austere origins. Jewish religion had banned images, yet Catholics decorated their churches with figures of Christ and the Virgin Mary, saints and martyrs amid rich trappings. During the Reformation an attempt was made to recapture the early simplicity. Also the focus of attention became the preacher rather than the altar.

the papacy was a foreign and unfriendly institution. Some heretics could draw also on social unrest; no Christian could forget what the Bible had to say about the injustices of life.

Still, the followers of Wyclif and Hus, 'Lollards' and 'Hussites' as they were called, were harried and chased by the authorities. It was not they who were to pull down the Church they often criticized, but which was still very strong in 1500 and by no means in much worse shape then than at earlier times, even if we seem suddenly to hear more about what is going wrong. Her influence was still taken for granted at every level of society, controlling, moulding, setting in familiar grooves and patterns the accidents of each individual's life, watching over him from the cradle to the grave. Religion was so tangled with everyday life that their separation was almost unthinkable. In most villages and little towns, for instance, there was no other public building than the Church; it is not surprising that people met in it for community business, and for amusement, at 'church-ales' and on feast days (when even dances were held in it).

Being mixed up in the everyday world was not always good for the Church. Bishops who played a prominent part in the affairs of their rulers had always been in danger of being too busy doing that to be good bishops. The great Cardinal Wolsey, archbishop of York and favourite of the English Henry VIII, never visited his see until sent there in disgrace after falling from favour and power. At the very centre of the Church, the popes themselves often seemed to worry too much about their position as temporal princes. Because the papal throne and the papal bureaucracy had both fallen more or less entirely into Italian hands, foreigners especially felt this. Pluralism – holding more than one office and neglecting them while drawing the pay for them – was another problem the Church had long faced and did not seem to be able to put right. One reason was that for all the grandeur of the way many bishops and abbots lived, for all the extravagance of the papal court at Rome ('Since God has given us the papacy', one pope is supposed to have said, 'let us enjoy it'), there never seemed to be enough money to go round and, as a result, jobs had to be dished out to reward services. Poverty created other difficulties too. Admittedly it was unusual for a pope to go so far as Sixtus IV, who was finally reduced to pawning the papal tiara, but using juridical and spiritual power to increase papal revenues was an old complaint, and it had its roots in the need to find revenue.

A pamphlet of 1521, attributed to Luther, illustrated by pairs of woodcuts contrasting Christ's humility with the pope's pomp and power. In the first of this pair Christ is shown washing and kissing Peter's feet; in the second the pope accepts similar homage from a king.

In the foreground of this picture by Holbein, are Monks selling indulgences; at the back, Leo X is being presented with some of the proceeds of the sale. Indulgences were usually sold along with a penance, but the pope was so anxious to collect the money to build St Peter's that the penances were often waived.

Pope Sixtus IV giving an audience to the Vatican's new librarian. Standing behind them are the pope's four nephews, one of whom became Pope Julius II.

Money was short at the level of the parish, too. Priests became more rigorous about collecting their tithes – the portion of the parishioners' produce (usually about a tenth or twelfth) to which they were entitled. This led to resentment and resistance which then tempted churchmen into trying to secure their rights by threatening to refuse people the sacraments – to excommunicate them – if they did not pay up. This was a serious business when men believed they might burn in hell for ever as a result. Finally, poverty was also a cause of clerical ignorance (though not the only one). The standard of education among the clergy had improved since the twelfth century (this owed much to the universities) but many parish priests in 1500 were hardly less ignorant and superstitious than their parishioners.

Against this background, when the papacy began to build a great new cathedral at Rome – the St Peter's which still stands there – it had to find new ways to raise money. One of these ways was licensing salesmen of 'indulgences'. These were preachers who, in return for a contribution to the funds needed for St Peter's, gave the pope's assurance that subscribers would be let off a certain amount of time in Purgatory, that part of the after-world in which the soul was believed to be purged and cleansed of its worldly wickedness before passing to heaven.

Indulgences unexpectedly provided the spark for the religious revolution. In 1517 a German monk, Martin Luther, decided to protest against them, together with several other papal practices. Like the good old-fashioned scholar he was, he followed tradition by posting his arguments in a set of ninety-five 'theses' for debate on the door of the castle church in Wittenberg, the town where he was a professor at the university. Here began the Protestant Reformation. Soon his arguments were translated from their original Latin into German. They ran through Germany like wild-fire – this was the age of print and so they had a wider audience than had earlier criticisms of the papacy. Because of this, Luther became one of the makers of world history.

Luther had the temperament for the task. He was a Saxon, the son of peasants, impulsive and passionate, who at the age of twenty-one became a monk after an emotional upheaval which took place one day when a thunder-

Luther's beliefs not only reached his countrymen through pamphlets but also through his powerful preaching. He is shown here in a characteristic pose.

storm broke on him as he was trudging along the highway. Overcome by terror and a feeling of his own sinfulness which made him sure he was fit only to go to hell if he was struck by lightning and killed, Luther suddenly felt the conviction that God cared for him and would save him. It was rather like St Paul's conversion on the road to Damascus in its suddenness and violence. Luther's first celebration of Mass was another overwhelming experience, so convinced was he of his personal unworthiness to be a priest. Later he was to believe Satan appeared to him – and he even threw his inkpot at him. Furthermore Luther's nature was such that, when convinced he was right, he was immovable and this is why his views had such an impact on history. Germany may have been ripe for Luther, but the Reformation would not have been what it was without him.

Enormous dislike of the Italian papacy waited to be tapped in Germany. Luther turned to writing and preaching with a will when the primate of Germany, the archbishop of Mainz, tried to silence him. He awoke a huge response. His fellow-monks abandoned him, but his university stood by him and so did the ruler of Saxony, the state he lived in. Eventually his writings divided Germans into those who came to be called 'Lutherans' (though he was first called a 'Hussite') and those who stood by the pope and the emperor. Support came to him not only from clergy who disapproved of the teaching and practice of the Roman clergy, but from humble folk with grievances against tithe-gatherers and church courts, from greedy princes who coveted the wealth of the Church, and from others who simply took his side because their traditional or habitual rivals came out against him.

Luther in the end set out his views in the form of new theological doctrines – that is to say, statements about the beliefs a Christian ought to hold in order to be sure that he really was a Christian and that he would be saved

Allegory, in pictures as well as words, was often used for propaganda in the disputes between Catholics and Protestants. In this painting, alluding to a Biblical parable, the English archbishop, Cranmer, points to the Catholics, on the left, destroying the Lord's vineyard and being paid off by Christ, while, on the right, Luther and his followers do the work as it should be done.

Although this could be the tonsured head of any monk, it is generally considered to be an anti-Lutheran picture, suggesting that Luther's sermons have been dictated to him by the devil.

after death from Hell. And here he did something very important, because he said that the Church itself and even attendance at the sacraments was not absolutely necessary to salvation, but that men might be saved if they had faith in Jesus Christ. He said a great deal more too, and much of it is very difficult to understand. The central point of his teaching, though, was that in the last resort you could still hope to be saved even without the Church, by simply relying on your own private relationship with God. It has been said that he dethroned the pope and enthroned the Bible, God's Word which every believer could consult without the Church coming between him and it. A view putting such stress on the individual conscience was revolutionary. Not surprisingly, Luther was excommunicated, but he went on preaching and won wider and wider support.

The political quarrels Luther's teaching aroused between Germany's rulers resulted in wars and revolts. After a long period of turmoil, a general settlement had to be made. By the peace of Augsburg of 1555 (nine years after Luther's death) it was agreed that Germany should be divided between Catholic and Protestant (the word had come into use after the signing of a 'Protestation' against the papacy in 1529). Which religion prevailed in

each state was to be the decision of its ruler. Thus yet another division was introduced into that divided land. The emperor Charles V had to accept this; it was the only way of getting peace in Germany, though he had struggled against the Reformers. For the first time Christian princes and churchmen recognized that there might be more than one source of religious authority and more than one recognized Church inside western Christendom. This is why, more than any other event, the Reformation can be seen as the true end of the Middle Ages in Europe and a religious revolution.

Something of which Luther himself disapproved had already begun to happen by then. Protestantism tended to fragment, as more and more people began to make up their own minds about religious questions. Other 'Protestants' than those who shared his views had soon appeared. The most important came from Switzerland, where a Frenchman, John Calvin, who had broken with Catholicism began to preach in the 1530s. He had great success at Geneva, and set up there a 'theocratic' state – that is, one governed by the godly

A Calvinist church, where decoration and imagery have been totally rejected. The pulpit and the words of the preacher have the undivided attention of the congregation.

(the Calvinists). Geneva was not a place for the easy-going. Heresy was punished by death; and though that was not surprising in those days, it was distinctly more ferocious to impose the death penalty (as Calvin did) for going off with someone else's wife or husband.

Calvinism also had great success in France, the Netherlands and Scotland, whereas, except in Scandinavia, Lutheranism did not for a long time spread much beyond the German lands where it had been born. The result, in any case, was further division – there were now two Protestant Europes and a Catholic one, as well as several minor Protestant sects.

One country whose change to Protestantism was to be particularly important for the future was England. In that country many of the forces operating elsewhere in favour of throwing off allegiance to the papacy were at work, and so was a diplomatic and personal one, the wish of Henry VIII to get rid of a queen who was not able to give him a son and heir. Yet Henry VIII was a loyal son of the Church who had actually written a book against Luther which earned him the papal title of 'Defender of the Faith', a title still borne by his descendant today. It is very likely that he would have been able to get his marriage to his queen 'annulled' – that is, deemed not to have been a proper marriage – by the pope, had she not

been aunt to the emperor Charles V, whose support was needed by the Church against the German heretics. So the papacy would not help, Henry quarrelled with the pope, England broke away from allegiance to Rome, and the lands of the English monasteries were seized by the Crown. Some Englishmen who were sympathetic to Luther also hoped to make the English Church Lutheran, but this did not happen.

Protestantism's success forced change on the Roman Catholic Church. Whatever hopes Roman Catholics might have of returning to the former state of affairs, they would have to live for the foreseeable future in a Europe where there were other claimants to the name of 'Christian'. One effect was that Roman Catholicism became more rigid and intransigent – or, if you put it in a different way, better disciplined and more orderly. This was the 'Counter-Reformation'. Several forces helped but the most important of them was a general Council of the Church which opened at Trent in north Italy in 1545 and sat, on and off, until 1563. It redefined much of the Church's doctrine, laid down new regulations for the training of priests and asserted papal authority. Putting its decisions into practice was made a little easier by the work of a remarkable Spaniard, Ignatius Loyola, who had founded a

Foxe's Book of Martyrs *was one of the most important Protestant propaganda works. Protestants persecuted, too, and the torments shown in Foxe's book were sometimes inflicted by Protestants on Catholics. On the whole, though, the Protestants had the best of the propaganda battle about persecution.*

new order of clergy to serve the papacy, the Society of Jesus, or 'Jesuits'. The Jesuits, sanctioned in 1540 and bound by a special vow of obedience to the pope himself, were carefully trained as an elite corps of teachers and missionaries (Loyola was especially concerned to evangelize the newly discovered pagan lands). More than any other clergy they embodied the combative, unyielding spirit of the Counter-Reformation. This matched Loyola's temper, for he had been a soldier and always seems to have seen his Society in very military terms; Jesuits were sometimes spoken of as the 'militia' of the Church. Together with the Inquisition, an old institution for the pursuit of heresy which became the final court of appeal in heresy trials in 1542, and the 'Index' of prohibited books first issued in 1557, the Jesuits were part of a new armoury of weapons for the papacy, which now became very authoritarian.

Reformation and Counter-Reformation divided Europeans bitterly. The Orthodox world of the east was little affected, but everywhere in what had been Catholic Europe there were for more than a century religious struggles. Some countries successfully persecuted minorities right out of existence: Spain and (in large measure) Italy thus remained strongholds of the Counter-Reformation. Rulers usually made up their minds for themselves and their subjects sometimes fell in with their decisions. Foreigners occasionally tried to intervene. England had the Channel to protect her, and was in less danger from abroad than Germany or France. Yet religion was not the only explanation of the so-called 'religious wars' which devastated so much of Europe between 1550 and 1648. Sometimes, as in France, what was really going on was a struggle for dominance between great aristocratic families who identified themselves with different

The infamous massacre of St Bartholomew's Day in 1572. Many Huguenots were in Paris to celebrate the wedding of the Protestant Henry of Navarre, later Henry IV, to the Catholic Margaret, daughter of Henry II and Catherine de Medici. The queen, fearing the growing power of the Huguenots, had as many as possible murdered before dawn.

religious parties. In the end a representative of a Protestant family came out on top – as the king Henry IV – but did so by changing his religion to Catholicism. So the French monarchy stayed Catholic, though many 'Huguenots' (Protestant Frenchmen) for a long time enjoyed special rights of self-defence and had fortified towns where they could practise their own religion.

In the Netherlands, which were under Spanish rule, religion gradually transformed a rebellion which had been started by the local nobility who wanted more local self-government. In the end the aristocratic leaders of the southern provinces (modern Belgium) felt they had better stay Catholic and under Spanish rule, while the northern provinces (roughly, the modern kingdom of the Netherlands) identified themselves with Protestantism, even though they contained a large Catholic population. After a long struggle – the Dutch call it the 'Eighty Years' War' – Europe found that a new country had come into existence, the United Provinces, a little federation of tiny republics, led by Holland, within which religious toleration was practised.

The worst abuse of religion for political ends was in Germany. The religious quarrels settled at Augsburg broke out again when a seventeenth-century Habsburg emperor, strongly imbued with Counter-Reformation principles, tried again to advance Catholicism. The outcome was the appalling 'Thirty Years' War' – it raged from 1618 to 1648 – which was ruthlessly exploited by outsiders for their own interests, so that religious questions were lost to sight in the carnage. At one moment a French cardinal of the Church was allied to a Protestant Swedish king to thwart the interests of the Catholic Habsburgs. Meanwhile the Germans suffered as armies marched back and forth over their country leaving misery in their wake, and spreading disease and famine. Some areas were virtually depopulated; once-prosperous towns disappeared.

In the end there had to be another compromise. But the peace of Westphalia, which ended the war in 1648, opened a new era. Although even then many people still thought of religion as well-worth fighting over and certainly as something which justified murdering or torturing your neighbours (much as many people think today that political ideals do), statesmen for the most part began to take more account of other matters in dealing with one another. The world became a tiny bit more civilized when they turned their attention back to arguments about trade and territory, and away from religion. Europe by then, in the second half of the seventeenth century, was divided into states, most of which did not officially tolerate more than one dominant religion, but in some of which a fair degree of tolerance was practised. And there were two countries – England and the United Provinces – where a very large measure of religious freedom was available to those who did not conform to the established Church, even if they did not enjoy all the privileges of its members.

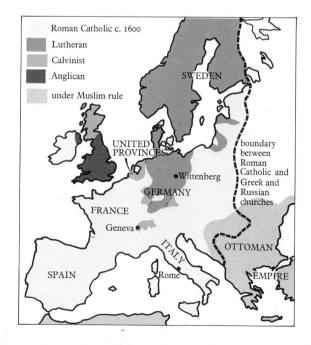

Roman Catholic c. 1600
Lutheran
Calvinist
Anglican
under Muslim rule

SWEDEN
UNITED PROVINCES
Wittenberg
GERMANY
FRANCE
Geneva
ITALY
SPAIN
Rome
OTTOMAN EMPIRE

boundary between Roman Catholic and Greek and Russian churches

Europe's new political patterns

Sixteenth-century monarchs did not think of themselves as doing anything very new and often behaved in very 'medieval' ways or at least ones which we should find somewhat surprising in modern rulers. French kings still set off to invade Italy very much in the spirit (they thought) of the chivalrous knights of old, while Henry VIII of England turned up in 1520 to a spectacular diplomatic meeting in Flanders – the Field of the Cloth of Gold – which was run much as a traditional medieval social occasion, with tournaments and jousting. Kings still fought, for the most part, for the advancement of their own family's in-

A detail from 'The Field of the Cloth of Gold' painted to commemorate Henry VIII of England's meeting with Francis I of France in 1520. The meeting had been arranged for the two kings to conclude peace between their countries, but became a contest between the two monarchs, each trying to outdo the other in magnificence. No alliance was made, and war broke out in 1522.

terests rather than those of the people over whom they ruled. As for those at a lower level of public life, noblemen still fought back hard when they thought that kings were encroaching on the independence or dignity they were entitled to by custom. Medieval representative bodies (one of them was the English parliament) also still had a long life ahead of them in some countries.

Yet great political changes were coming. Though these were not always complete even by 1800, the old 'feudal' arrangements which once governed almost the whole of Europe had by then ceased to matter everywhere west of the Rhine and in some of the lands to the east of it. The process behind this had begun far back in the Middle Ages. Towns had never really fitted into feudal society and they had grown greatly in size and importance since 1100. More and more of the tradesmen and merchants who lived in them were independent men, wealthier than most nobles. In the later

Middle Ages too countrymen often found themselves working for wages and came to demand the freedom to do so for whomever they liked. Such pressures on traditional ways only changed society very slowly and were very complicated, but they already made it impossible by 1500 to think only in 'feudal' terms.

Kings, for all their conservatism, were especially likely to be impatient with some of the old feudal ways. They wanted to rule – and that really meant to tax – their subjects without interference from anybody else. They employed lawyers to think up ways of undermining the old arrangements, professional soldiers to make sure that they could squash vassals if they stepped out of line, and civil servants to make sure that government would go on even if local bigwigs turned sour. Moreover as time went by they paid less and less attention to their own supposed duties to other magnates; though he was theoretically top dog among Europe's rulers, they treated the Holy Roman Emperor, for example, simply like any other prince, intent on promoting the interests of his own dynasty just as they were.

Competition with one another made it all the more important for kings to keep a strong grip on their domains, and made them even more eager to break old-fashioned obstacles to their power. This helped the slow emergence of something people take for granted nowadays, the idea of 'sovereignty'. In essence this means that (as is now held) within a given area there is only one ultimate law-making authority. This idea began to spread in the sixteenth century. No one, some felt, whether emperor or pope, had the right to interfere between a sovereign (whether a single prince or a body like the senate of Venice did not matter) and his own subjects. It was a long time, it is true, before this idea was accepted completely and everywhere, and people went on finding it very difficult to agree with the idea that the sovereign could do anything (even something which cut across the laws of God, for example), but by 1800 the theory that the state or its ruler was the over-riding source of law was accepted throughout most of Europe, even if relics of the older ideas still lingered on.

So kings and princes grew more powerful, and there emerged what has been called 'absolute' monarchy. The first great example was Spain. Under Philip II, the son of Charles V, who had left to Philip the Spanish part of the Habsburg lands when he abdicated in 1556, Spanish government was centralized to an astonishing degree. Almost every important decision, whether it was about negotiations

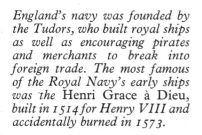

England's navy was founded by the Tudors, who built royal ships as well as encouraging pirates and merchants to break into foreign trade. The most famous of the Royal Navy's early ships was the Henri Grace à Dieu, *built in 1514 for Henry VIII and accidentally burned in 1573.*

with other European states, the taxes to be paid in the Spanish Netherlands or the appointment of a new official in the Spanish empire in the Americas, was in theory settled by the king. In the huge monastery-palace which he built not far from Madrid, El Escorial, the paper piled up as Philip tried to run a world-wide empire, direct the economy of Spain, root out heresy in his dominions and make them wholly Christian, and keep an eye on everything going on by means of a huge spy system – all from his study. It was too much to hope for. In the end he failed, but Spain, which was also the military and naval champion of the Counter-Reformation, was an outstanding example of what absolutism could mean in practice.

Perhaps the most spectacularly successful of absolute kings was Louis XIV, who ruled France from 1660 (he had legally been king since 1643, when he was five) to 1715. Once he had taken over the actual powers of government himself, he pitched the claims of

The south façade of El Escorial and its reservoir.

Monarchs of the sixteenth and seventeenth centuries built grand palaces to reinforce their prestige as well as to provide attractive living quarters for themselves and their courtiers. The most splendid example of such combinations of diplomacy, administration and beauty is Versailles, conceived and built by Louis XIV throughout his reign.

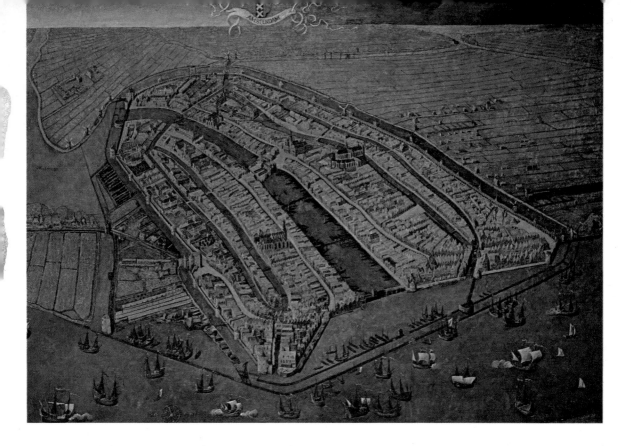

Amsterdam as it appeared in 1538.

monarchy higher than any other seventeenth-century king. Under him, there was no more trouble from the French nobility and the privileges of the Huguenots were taken away. Higher taxation supported a more powerful army than ever before and a successful run of conquests (at least for the first half of his reign). But there were limits even to Louis's power; he was careful not to antagonize his nobles.

Not all European states developed in this direction. The outstanding exceptions were the Dutch United Provinces and England. In the first case, it sometimes looked as if the Dutch could have done with rather more centralization and strong government, because rivalries between different provinces often made it very difficult for them to cooperate against pressure from the outside. But this was a price paid for having more freedom than was perhaps to be found anywhere else. This freedom was basically a matter of defending the independence of action of the relatively small ruling groups of rich citizens who dominated the government of each state. The most important were the merchant rulers of Amsterdam, capital of the province of Holland and centre of Dutch commercial life. But because their outlook on most matters was similar to that of the majority of those they ruled, and because their economic interests often coincided with those of poorer people – everyone suffered, for example, if business was bad in Amsterdam, not just the rich – and because they were very anxious to do nothing which would diminish their freedom to trade and make money, the care of the rich to preserve the freedom of the states assured freedom for the individual citizen. They were remarkably successful during most of the seventeenth century, though they had to fight hard against Louis XIV (who combined his dislike of them as republicans with a liking for their tulips, of which he bought millions each year). By the eighteenth century, partly because of the strains this imposed, the Dutch were entering a period of decline and were never again to be quite such an important world-power as they had been in the previous hundred years.

The English story was very different. It looked for a time as if the early Tudors might well develop a strong centralizing monarchy like those in Europe. They had the oldest national monarchical tradition in Europe to draw on and a national feeling in many ways more developed than elsewhere behind it. These made it easier for Henry VIII to carry out his nationalization of the Church in England; Protestantism became identified with national feeling in England as it did nowhere else except in Germany. Yet Henry VIII had turned to another old institution, parliament, to make the necessary laws. This was very important for the future. There were bodies rather like parliaments in other countries, but almost everywhere in the next couple of centuries they went down before the demands of absolutism; instead, the English parliament grew stronger and stronger. Why was this?

The answer is complicated, but much of it was the work of the Tudors, though they probably would not have wished it to be. When Henry asked parliament to pass laws about the fate of the Church, he was implying that they had a right to legislate on such an important matter; that made it very difficult for later kings to act in similar matters without parliament's support. Another factor was the uncertainty of the succession (none of Henry's children had offspring). The reign of Elizabeth I is now often seen as a great age, and so it was, yet the queen was for a long time insecure and afraid she might lose her throne (and perhaps her head: hence she cut off that of one possible rival, Mary Queen of Scots). The European situation was against her, and other possible claimants to the throne had a good chance of foreign support. She was therefore careful not

Two English monarchs: Elizabeth I being carried through the street by her courtiers, and an engraving showing the execution of King Charles I, published in Dutch and German pamphlets. He is shown three times: the central figure about to kneel at the block, on the right, having been beheaded and, above, ascending to glory as a martyr. Europeans were horrified by the idea of trying and executing a king, and the witnesses of the execution are shown overcome by it.

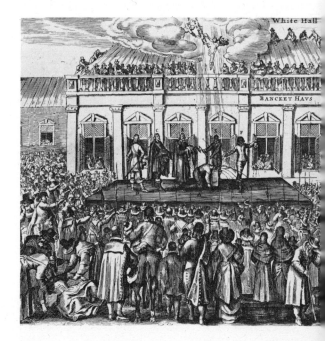

to antagonize her subjects. One of the ways in which they made themselves heard was through parliament, which voted taxes. It gradually became clear that the monarchy could not levy taxes without parliament's approval of the purposes for which they were raised.

'Good Queen Bess' was so successful at handling people that she was able to conceal much of this. Her more stupid successors, the first two Stuart kings, were not, possibly in part because James I was a Scotsman who did not much like or understand ways Englishmen had grown used to under the Tudors. Under him and his son, the Crown's relations with parliament broke down. In the middle of the seventeenth century, a great civil war finally settled that England would not develop towards continental absolutism (though, oddly, the country was for a time ruled as a republic by someone with powers very like a dictator's, the 'Lord Protector', Oliver Cromwell). The defeat of absolute monarchy was confirmed in 1688, when an almost bloodless upheaval, the 'Glorious Revolution', pushed off the throne the last Stuart king, James II, because it was believed that he was trying to reverse the trend of the last hundred and fifty years by creating an unchecked monarchy to establish Catholicism again in England.

After that, England was really ruled by its

After the execution of Charles I, Cromwell crushed the Scottish allies of Charles II in the battle of Dunbar (1650). This medal struck to commemorate his victory shows Cromwell.

landowners, who dominated parliament. But, just as the interests of the ruling rich in the Dutch republic often turned out to be the interests of many other people too, so England's rulers looked after national interests pretty well. After all, agriculture was England's main industry; what was good for the landlord and the farmer was likely to be good for the country. Furthermore other interests – bankers' and merchants', for example – were not ignored. They might grumble about policies, but government usually took account of their views. Gradually Englishmen began to feel there was a connection between obvious advantages they enjoyed – personal freedom, equality before the law, Protestantism, safeguards against absolute monarchy – and the growing wealth of the country. After 1660 or thereabouts, though there were many setbacks on the way, there could be no doubt that Englishmen found it easier to stand by the constitution.

Already in the eighteenth century many Europeans admired England for her freedom. By this, they did not mean only that she was ruled by elected representatives (even if mainly chosen by landowners) and aristocrats, instead of by a despotic monarch, but that Englishmen were much freer from interference with their private lives than many Europeans. It was harder to keep them locked up without trial, for example, than elsewhere, and Englishmen were not used to having their homes entered and searched without a magistrate's warrant. Rank was very important in English society, but, if a great lord committed a crime, he could be brought before a court like anyone else. All this was very strange and admirable to many people who lived on the continent. Yet it too was largely the consequence of England being ruled by landowners who wanted to protect themselves and thought the best way to do so was by putting behind such privileges the force of laws which only parliament could change. This alternative to absolutism is often called 'constitutionalism'.

The changing European outlook

It is only too easy to give too much historical attention to the ideas of very untypical men, the leading writers, scholars and scientists of an age. Of course we must study them in order to explain how ideas, later of enormous importance, first arose and were developed – but in their own day they may actually have influenced only very small numbers of people. Yet, because their ideas are the ones which get written down in books which survive, they tend to dominate the story of what people were 'really' thinking about at a particular time. This is a distortion. We now live in an age when science has great prestige and is obviously doing things all around us which demonstrate its power to handle the natural world, yet many Europeans (to say nothing of others) still believe that crossing fingers and not walking under ladders will ward off bad luck, or that the astrologers who write in newspapers can 'predict' the future course of events from the stars. When trying to pin down the ways in which the world of ideas lived in by Europeans changed from one which took certain ideas for granted to one which took others for granted, we have to be very careful not to forget the qualifications which there is not space and time enough to spell out.

One thing which changed a lot by 1800 was the way that educated Europeans were likely to think about the past. Even in 1500, a few learned men had suggested that history made better sense if you thought of what was then happening as being quite unlike what had preceded it. We know they were thinking like this because they used special phrases to indicate that between then and the classical antiquity of the Greeks and Romans lay an in-between time different from either, for which an old Latin term existed and could be used: *medium aevum*. In the sixteenth century writers provided equivalents in other European languages too: *mitler jare* in old German, *moyen aage* in old French, and finally 'Middle Age' or 'Middle Ages' in English.

By 1800 this idea was pretty much taken for granted by the educated. It has had a good run ever since. It still seems sensible to say that 'medieval' Europe was in important ways very different from what came next, even if we do not use that term in the same way as the men who invented the idea. For the most part they

Until recently most libraries were owned by rich individuals or institutions such as monasteries or universities. Only a few were open to the public, as was this one, founded in Florence by Lorenzo the Magnificent in the fifteenth century and re-founded as a public library in 1571 in a building by Michelangelo. The books were either stored flat or stood on lecterns.

were only interested in the classical past and saw themselves on one side of a great chasm – the Middle Ages – which separated them from it. But they also thought of themselves as engaged in recovering the classical past by reviving the study of Greek and Latin and by reminding people of its standards and achievements. They did not, that is to say, claim to be doing something wholly new. This is why some of them had the idea that they were taking part in what we call (from a French word) the 'Renaissance' – it meant '*re*birth' of arts and learning, not 'birth', for that, they thought, had already happened long ago.

Within a fairly short time, though, people began to think rather differently of the new age they lived in. They began to stress just how new and completely different it was from

earlier history. Often they made the point by emphasizing how bad, gloomy and backward the past had been, especially the Middle Ages, which they depicted as superstitious and barbaric – 'monkish' was a favourite word for it. Not everyone agreed. There were great debates about whether mankind had done finer things in ancient times, and, as time passed, about whether other civilizations (the Chinese was the most popular candidate) had reached greater heights. And the changes of view were not in the end entirely in one direction. In the early nineteenth century people were already beginning to feel that there was more to the

St Augustine, portrayed by the Florentine painter Botticelli, was one of the greatest religious teachers of the Latin world. His writings strongly influenced medieval theology and politics. His teachings on grace and predestination were taken up by Luther and Calvin. His appeal to the men of the Renaissance lay in his success in combining scholarly and spiritual ideals.

An illustration from a psalter written for Henry VIII, showing him reading in his bedroom. The influence of the Italian Renaissance can be seen in the furniture as well as in the view through the arch. Henry VIII was often portrayed as the 'new', Renaissance man – the all-rounder as proficient in the arts and learning as in athletics and statesmanship.

Middle Ages than their critics allowed, and that they were in some ways to be admired.

From a historian's point of view this was all to the good. What was happening was that more people were coming to look at the past more carefully, however far short of seeing its true nature they still were. But, behind this, something had been going on in these three centuries which was one of the most important changes ever to occur in the outlook of Europeans. The gist of it was that large numbers of them became convinced that the history of mankind was moving *forward*, that it showed a pattern of continuing *progress*. They came to

Men the Renaissance admired – a painter, astronomers, a sculptor, mathematicians and a musician – portrayed in a German woodcut.

believe that they were more advanced in civilization, taste, knowledge, science, art than any earlier age and perhaps even that their successors would be more advanced still. The world, in short, was getting better all the time. This was a huge break with medieval views which had often stressed either how much worse things were getting or that, anyway, they could not be changed.

Some of the roots of such a change in outlook lay in the revival of classical learning. It had in fact begun long before 1500. The Renaissance, however we define it, was going strong before the end of the fourteenth century. But its main developments certainly became most widely known and more generally accepted in the sixteenth century. It was then that the admirers of classical literature and art made their biggest claims for what they admired. A respect for Greece and Rome had in the past been thought to be reconcilable with Christianity. But gradually some of the 'humanists', as they were called, began to emphasize things about classical antiquity which had nothing to do with Christianity and might even be opposed to it. To take a simple example: Christianity said a great deal about the virtues of turning the other cheek, and showing meekness and humility, but this was not the sort of behaviour which was admired by the Greeks and Romans, whose literature and history were full of examples of full-blooded derring-do. One effect of the revival of classical learning therefore was to suggest to some people that non-Christian standards and values might have much to be said for them. This was one way in which the Renaissance contributed to the sense of a break with the past and to the weakening of ideas which had held European culture together for centuries. Like the Protestant Reformation it made for a more secular, more diversified civilization.

Still, this must not be overstressed. Humanists who admired pagan virtues and put them before those of Christianity were a minority, and a small one at that, within the world of educated men – which was itself a minority within Europe as a whole. Most humanists found a love of classical learning quite compatible with their Christian beliefs. The most famous of them all, perhaps, was the Dutchman, Erasmus of Rotterdam, and his main purpose in perfecting his learning was to use it to provide good texts of the New Testament and the works of the Fathers of the Church.

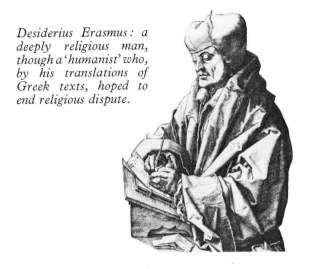

Desiderius Erasmus: a deeply religious man, though a 'humanist' who, by his translations of Greek texts, hoped to end religious dispute.

Below: part of the title page for Sir Thomas More's Utopia, *which appeared in 1516. Utopia was an imaginary island where, according to More, in a society based on communal ownership, men and women had equal rights.*

The Italian Renaissance

Every European country west of Russia felt in some measure the direct influence of the Renaissance. Most of them were to contribute something important to it, too. Italy, though, was its real centre and heart. From about 1350 to 1450 many more scholars, artists, scientists and poets lived in the cities of Italy than in any other country. The rest of Europe went to school to Italy, as it were, to learn how to copy the beautiful and clever things they could find there.

The Italians, too, felt they had much to learn, but looked to the classical past of Greece and Rome as the place where they would learn it. The Renaissance had its roots in discovering again part of Europe's past which had been overshadowed by Christian civilization during the Middle Ages. Raphael glorified the great philosophers of Greece in his *School of Athens* and humanist writers imitated the style of the Roman Cicero in order to produce elegant Latin. The 'rebirth' of classical learning, indeed, was what gives the Renaissance its name, for *Rinascimento* – the Italian word for 'rebirth' – is the word translated into French as *Renaissance* and adopted by the English. But the most striking evidence of

what the Renaissance did is still its art. In painting, sculpture, engraving, architecture, music, and poetry it has left a vast collection of beautiful creations which have for centuries shaped men's ideas of what beauty should be. This art came to a climax in the late fifteenth and early sixteenth centuries, the age of – among others – Michelangelo, sculptor, painter, architect and poet; of Raphael, painter and architect; and of Leonardo da Vinci, painter, engineer, architect, sculptor and scientist. The men of the Renaissance admired such all-rounders. At the nobles' courts, a young man was expected to be able to write verses or sing part-songs and to have a taste for beautiful objects, as well as be a good fencer or horseman. The Renaissance gave people a new idea of human excellence. They came to see man as a creature of greater potential here on earth than had been thought in the middle Ages. In Michelangelo's painting of the *Creation of Adam*, the father of the human race is a gigantic, heroic figure, dwarfing in power and dramatic effect even his creator, whose finger gives him life.

School of Athens, *a fresco by Raphael.*

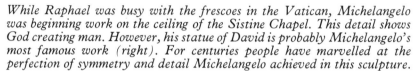

While Raphael was busy with the frescoes in the Vatican, Michelangelo was beginning work on the ceiling of the Sistine Chapel. This detail shows God creating man. However, his statue of David is probably Michelangelo's most famous work (right). For centuries people have marvelled at the perfection of symmetry and detail Michelangelo achieved in this sculpture.

By returning to the clear-cut, classical lines of ancient Greece, Bramante reached a landmark in the history of Renaissance architecture, especially in the design of the Tempietto as a monument to mark the supposed spot of St Peter's crucifixion in Rome.

Leonardo da Vinci is known throughout the world for his painting of the Mona Lisa, but he left behind a mass of work in many different fields. For example, he carried out careful studies of human anatomy (as we can see from this sketch he made of a skull) and the many notes and diagrams he left behind indicate that he even came near to inventing a flying machine.

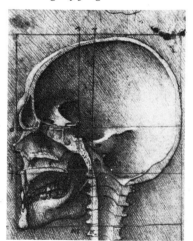

The age of print

A new medium was available to the humanists for spreading their ideas: print. Thanks to the bringing together of movable metal type, oil-based inks and better presses in the fifteenth century, Erasmus's editions of the New Testament in Greek, for example, could reach many more people more quickly than the work of earlier scholars. In this case it gave them a text which was much more accurate than any earlier one and therefore a much better basis for discussion of what the New Testament really meant.

But this example also illustrates another point: the New Testament was part of the Bible, and this was the book more frequently printed than any other in the early days of printing. This shows that it was by no means likely to be new and startling ideas which were put into print at first. It is easy to see why. People wanted books which had already been famous even when they had to be written out by hand – the Bible, works by great theologians and lawyers, famous texts by the ancient authors – not novelties. Nevertheless the existence of the printing-press was of huge importance in circulating new ideas among small numbers of those specially interested in them. The great accelerations in scientific advance in the seventeenth century, for example, could hardly have been possible without printing.

Other changes were connected with it too. Europe became a much more literate society between 1500 and 1800. Most Europeans still could not read even at the end of that time, but it was more common for the better-off to do so. Moreover even those who could not read shared some of the benefit. Those who could read often read aloud to them; it seems to have been the practice in parts of France, for example, for people to gather deliberately to hear someone read from story-books sold by pedlars, and in eighteenth-century England, people used to listen to newspapers read at the village inn.

What they heard read was written in the vernacular. Learned men continued to follow for a long time the practice of writing in Latin, the international language of scholarship. But more and more books were published in English, French, German, Italian, Spanish and other European languages. This often had an important effect on these languages. Just

In 1535 the first English-language Bible was printed (left). For two centuries the Bible was to be the most important single influence shaping English speech and literature, thanks to print. Scholars also benefited by being able to study basic mathematical problems set out before them in print, like this page from Euclid (right).

as the invention of writing in early times had helped to 'fix' language in certain ways, spreading common words and ways of using them, so printing further advanced this process. Spellings became more standardized, local words tended to survive only in speech, while printed language increasingly tended to be used over wide areas formerly separated by dialects and local idioms.

This process gained momentum as print began – very soon – to be used for things other than books. Broadsides, printed illustrations with explanations, newsletters, pamphlets and finally the true newspaper or periodical magazine all appeared before 1800. They by no means took the same form everywhere. A lot of difference was made from country to country by the law. Englishmen poured out political pamphlets in the seventeenth century, (one of the most famous was Milton's *Aeropagitica*, a great plea for liberty of the press), while France (because of censorship) was almost without them for another hundred years or so. Newspapers were in Germany from the seventeenth century onwards. But much more printed material was available everywhere in

1800 than three centuries earlier, and it is probably true that, whatever the quality of many of these publications and whatever their lack of novelty, a much wider discussion of ideas and events was going on than ever before.

This helped, in a very broad sense, to create a larger educated public, one beginning to get the idea, though slowly, that public affairs concerned it as well as its rulers. This was one reason why, as the end of these centuries approached, more and more demands were heard in countries other than England and the Dutch republic for people to have greater freedom to print and publish what they liked. It was in the eighteenth century that a famous French writer, Voltaire, said that, although he might disagree violently with what someone said, he would fight vigorously for his right to say it. By then, what such a statement meant was the right to print and publish opinions. This was to be something fought for in many countries by liberals in the nineteenth century and then – when the battle might have been thought to be won – again in the twentieth. But that is part of a story to be told later. Meanwhile it is worth recalling that even today democratic countries (such as Great Britain) have thought it necessary to limit freedom of publication in important areas – for instance, in the expression of views which appear to be racialist.

Soon, too, people were reading about local and national affairs in their news-sheets, and engravings were made available in prints like this German version of the Great Fire of London in 1666 (right).

Scientific revolutions

By the end of the seventeenth century printing had helped to create an international public of learned men who published scientific discoveries and observations in the form of 'proceedings' of learned bodies such as the Royal Society in England. This was undoubtedly one reason why what some people have spoken of as a 'Scientific Revolution' took place after 1500, though it might be better to emphasize that this 'Scientific Revolution' consisted of several big changes, and that these changes were by no means all closely connected.

Some of these great changes began simply with observations, as Renaissance artists worked out rules of perspective, for example, or doctors described in detail human anatomy, or map-makers tried to arrange and classify new geographical knowledge won by the voyages of the great discoverers.

Soon, though people went farther and began to make systematic experiments, one of the most important steps forward from medieval science, which was much too theoretical. One of the great advocates of doing so (though he was not listened to much in his own day) was

Lord Bacon, Lord Chancellor of England. He was a man of wide interests; some people believe he really wrote the plays of Shakespeare and, though this seems very unlikely, it tells us something about his reputation that it should be thought possible. Bacon was sure that, if scientific research were done systematically, it would give man enormous power over nature. He was right. He seems to have died in a highly appropriate way, catching cold one bitter March day while stuffing a fowl with snow to discover how refrigeration affected the flesh.

The feeling that experiments could be made to yield more fruitful results grew stronger as better instruments became available. Telescopes, microscopes, more accurate timekeepers all opened up new areas of investigation. But the fact that some instruments were developed before others also tended to channel science in specific directions. On the whole it was not until fairly late in these three centuries that chemistry began to make much of an advance, and only towards the eighteenth century did the biological sciences take their first

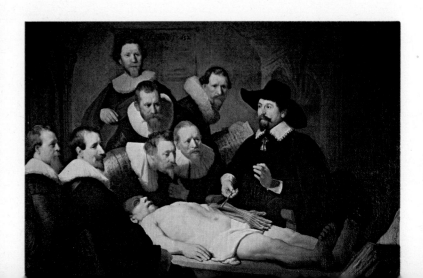

Dutch painting flowered in the seventeenth century with a realism which often seems very modern. This is one of several paintings by Rembrandt showing scientists studying human anatomy. The bodies used for such research were usually those of hanged criminals.

big steps forward. The most important sciences under way earlier than this were physics, astronomy and mathematics, and advances in them did more to change the way men looked at the world than any other scientific advances before the nineteenth century.

The first great name linked with this is that of Nicholas Copernicus, a Polish clergyman who in 1543 finished a book (dedicated to the pope) which provided a theoretical demonstration that the planets (including the earth) orbited about the sun. The theories of Ptolemy and commonsense both suggested this was nonsense: did not the sun rise each day and set

each evening? Clearly, then, the sun went round the earth. No one took much notice of what Copernicus said at first (though, interestingly, Protestant churchmen seem to have been quicker to condemn him than Catholics, who did not officially ban his doctrines until 1616), because it was not possible for a long time to demonstrate that this central idea of his book (which contained many other false ones) was true. Only when the telescope was available in the seventeenth century could Copernican astronomy become visible (its errors, it must be said, as well as its achievements).

The telescope was used in this way by an

Above: a diagram from Copernicus's book, depicting planetary orbits.

Right: the sixteenth-century Danish astronomer, Tycho Brahe, in the observatory specially built for him to house his scientific instruments, some of which appear in the pictures on the wall. They include his steel quadrant, which enabled him to measure the positions of the stars with an accuracy never achieved before.

Italian professor of physics and military engineering, Galileo Galilei. But he did much more than simply tell people to look through an instrument at what was going on in the skies. He also worked out the science needed to explain the Copernican universe. In the course of this he produced a new mathematics of the movement of bodies, statics and dynamics, building on the work of fourteenth-century scholars at Oxford who had formulated the first satisfactory law of acceleration.

The book Galileo published in 1632 with the title *A Dialogue on the two great systems of the world* (that is to say, the theories of Copernicus and those of Ptolemy) provoked an uproar. It led in the end to the trial of the author before the Inquisition in Rome where he recanted what he had said (though legend has it that even as he agreed that the sun went round the earth, which he agreed *was* the fixed centre of the universe, he muttered 'yet it *does* move'). But formal suppression of his book hardly mattered, for he had set out his views in full, and they were now public property.

Galileo's *Dialogue* has been hailed as the first outright statement of the Scientific Revolution because, whatever its author might say under pressure, the ideas in that book meant the end of the old views of the universe upheld by the Church and traceable back to Aristotle. Even simple men could see what problems this raised – what had happened to heaven? Where was God located? Furthermore Galileo's case advertised the fact that authority – believing something was true just because someone said so – had been worsted in debate by arguments based on observation and logical deduction. Galileo not only presented a picture of a universe of which the earth – and therefore man – was not the centre but merely one of several similar bodies, but also suggested it was possible to define its workings without mystical or religious explanations.

Galileo died in 1642. In the same year the greatest scientist of the century, Isaac Newton, was born in Lincolnshire. The achievement for which he is most famous is his demonstration that one force – gravity – sustained the physical universe. His theory of gravitation was the core of his most famous book, the *Principia Mathematica*, published in 1687 and said to have been fully understandable to only three or four other men of his time. It brought together the explanation of the heavens and

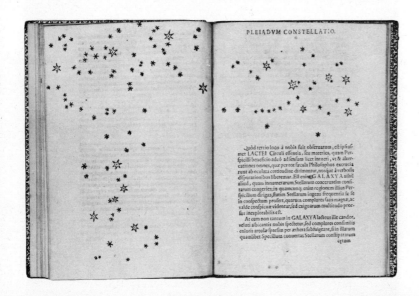

These pages, from Sidereus Nuncius (The Starry Messenger) *by Galileo and published in 1610, illustrate the 'new' stars revealed by the early telescope. On the left is the belt and sword of Orion, previously thought to be made up of only nine stars, and on the right the Pleiades, shown up to this date as a group of seven.*

the earth – astronomy and physics – and drew a picture of the universe which was to prove adequate for most purposes for the next two centuries. Newton did many other things too, for he was a man of vast and varied scientific interests and outstanding intellectual powers. (He was so obviously a genius that his own professor at Cambridge resigned his chair when his pupil was only twenty-seven so that Newton could have it.) Yet his discovery of a single physical law which seemed to explain so much is the main reason for his importance in the history of thought. Like Galileo, Newton changed the way laymen looked at the world. At last it began to seem that almost all its secrets might be unlocked by science – and if that was so, thought one or two adventurous people (though certainly not Newton, who was a very religious man), what need for priests and churchmen to explain it? What need, even, to talk about God as part of the explanation, since science might explain all of it by the discovery of further great regulating laws?

In the eighteenth century much more was heard of such ideas. Some men even went on to say that the world was a completely self-contained, mechanically determined system, that all that men had to explain and understand in order to live happy lives was the physical universe. For the first time (though only in the eyes of very few people) 'atheism' – the belief that there is no God – became respectable. It must never be forgotten that only a tiny minority of Europeans – themselves a minority in the world – would have thought like this in 1800. The overwhelming majority, even then, believed still in some sort of invisible world, some kind of God, some form of life after death – and many would still have believed in much cruder things, such as magic and witchcraft. Much of the ferocity of the religious wars of the sixteenth and seventeenth centuries had been due to the fact that people believed that great stakes were being played for; divine

punishment might fall on the country which allowed God's will to be thwarted by heretics. Witches and wizards had been harried and hunted, as people sought in them the explanation for misfortunes which befell them, and such ways of looking at the world persisted among the population at large. Still, at least educated men knew that some thinkers had pushed a long way down the road along which science (and some other signposts) seemed to point. That is why it is fair to say that the scientific ideas of the sixteenth and seventeenth centuries really did amount to a revolution in thought. After it, educated men were gradually ceasing to be satisfied with gazing at nature's wonders with bemused awe and the reflection that God had his own though mysterious reasons for creating them. Instead they sought increasingly to find ways of manipulating and exploiting nature. This was an attitude which was to spread much more widely in the next century.

Flamsteed House, named after John Flamsteed, the first Astronomer Royal, and part of the Old Royal Observatory in Greenwich, shortly after it was founded in 1675. The pole sticking out at an angle of forty-five degrees is in fact a long telescope.

Europe discovers the world

The sixteenth and seventeenth centuries were a great age of overseas adventure for Europeans. By 1700 the shape of all the main continents was pretty well known; only the outlines of eastern Australia and northern Siberia, and those of the far American north-west and Bering Strait region had not yet been mapped. Though huge unknown patches remained within Africa and Australia, world maps of a high degree of accuracy were available for the rest of the globe. If he took his chance of shipwreck, storm, piracy and disease, a traveller might put himself in the hands of a ship's captain with reasonable confidence; as far as navigation and seamanship could assure it, he could be delivered anywhere on the coasts of the world that he wished (and certainly at any of its ports) within three or four months.

This was a great advance on the situation two hundred years or so earlier. Columbus had died still arguing that his Caribbean discoveries were islands off the coast of Asia, so much was still then unknown. No European had then seen the Pacific or sailed directly to China, let alone gone round the world. Yet change had come very rapidly and at a quickening pace, once it began. The geographical and technical knowledge needed for overseas enterprises was cumulative: the more there was, the easier the next advance became.

A painting of Portuguese ships, from about 1520. The large ship in the foreground is probably the Santa Catarina do Monte Sinai, *one of the largest men-of-war of the day.*

Nevertheless some things did not change much for two or even three centuries. European ships grew bigger but, three hundred years after Columbus died, they still usually had square-rigged sails and were dependent on wind and tide. Lord Nelson, the great British admiral whose career came to its peak in 1805 when he was killed in action, would have found the *Golden Hind*, flagship of his Elizabethan predecessor, Francis Drake, uncomfortable, cramped and woefully without refinements the officers of his age took for granted. However, he would have known how to sail and navigate her. The principles and skill needed for mastering wind and water were much the same in 1500 as in 1800. The European ocean-going sailing ship was for the whole of these three centuries superior in sailing quality to most vessels available elsewhere. Its guns multiplied the fighting power of its

The magnetic properties of some iron oxides were first discovered in the eleventh century. Lodestones, as these pieces of metal came to be called, were used as early ships' compasses. The one shown above has been bound in brass.

The title page of a Dutch nautical manual translated into English. The text in the centre, promising the reader detailed information on sea routes and ports as well as the rules of navigation, is surrounded by illustrations of what would then have been the latest scientific aids to seamen.

crews. They could stand off from vessels built to grapple with the enemy and board him, and pound their opponents into submission from a distance instead. Even the noise of the guns helped, for it is said that, when the first European ship called at Canton, in south China, the greeting salute she fired caused a terrible fright.

What sent Europeans to sea? Not all European countries were represented among the sea-farers. Countries with Atlantic or North Sea coasts reaped the advantages of early enterprises – Portuguese, Spanish, French, English, Dutch and Danes were always to be foremost in them. Many Italian names can also be found in the early crews, a reminder of the old traditions of sea-borne trading of the Genoese and Venetians in the eastern Mediterranean in the Middle Ages. Eastern and central Europeans, though, did not figure in the first great phase of overseas enterprise. Nor did one or two peoples with easy access to the sea who might have been expected to – the Irish, for instance, or the Scots or Norwegians (though both of these were prominent in maritime commerce in later times).

Once the idea had caught on that there were big rewards to be won, rivalry and imitation played a big part. The story had begun with the search for a way round the Mediterranean barrier of Islam to Asia with its fabulous and rare products. The quest for new routes attracted people for many different reasons – for profit, above all, but also because of missionary prospects. Even simple curiosity played a part. Well before 1500 these motives had been reinforced by the discovery that the African coast, passed on the way to Asia itself, had something to offer – gold, ivory, slaves – and soon after that date by knowledge that the Americas offered land for colonists, booty for adventurers, mines for prospectors, marvels for the curious and souls for conversion to the Church. People saw there was more and more to be gained from going overseas.

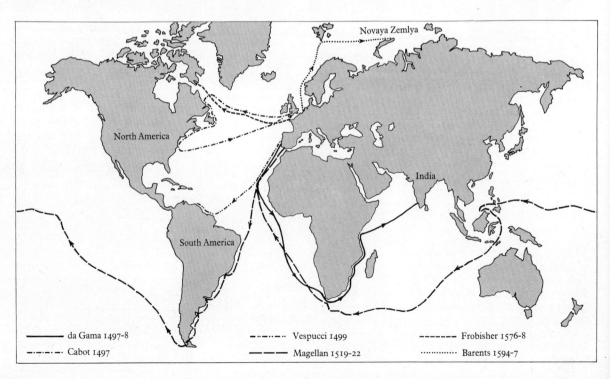

| —————— da Gama 1497-8 | —·—··— Vespucci 1499 | — — — — Frobisher 1576-8 |
| —·—·—· Cabot 1497 | — —— — Magellan 1519-22 | ·············· Barents 1594-7 |

Some of the hazards facing early explorers. The men attacking and being attacked by polar bears (above) are members of Barents's crew, the first Europeans known to have survived the Arctic winter. Below: sharks in the Indian Ocean.

The great voyages which mapped the world and brought back the first reports of new-found lands were essential to all that followed. Vasco da Gama reached India in 1498, the year when Sebastian Cabot, sailing out of Bristol, made his second voyage to a landfall on the coast of North America. Amerigo Vespucci in 1499 began the exploration of the coast of South America and eventually got as far south as the Falkland islands. In 1508 a Portuguese sailed into the Persian Gulf. In 1513 Balboa crossed the isthmus of Panama and Europeans looked for the first time at the Pacific. Then, in 1519, began what was to prove the greatest achievement of the early navigators: the Portuguese Magellan set out

from Seville and in the following year turned the tip of South America by the straits still named after him to sail into the vast unknown of the Pacific. In 1521 he was killed in the Ladrones islands, but one of his ships sailed on, via the Philippines and Timor, crossing the Indian Ocean, rounding Africa and making it back to Seville. Its Spanish commander, del Cano, was the first captain to sail round the world, thus showing that all the great oceans were interconnected. Men had known in theory that it could be done; now they knew it because someone had done it.

Before the century was out many other great voyages followed. Traders, missionaries and soldiers were soon into the Caribbean, the Indian Ocean, the South China Sea and the Pacific. More northerly waters remained unexplored for longer. In 1553 an English ship reached the site of what then became the Russian port of Archangel and returned with a letter from the Tsar to Mary Tudor. A series of English voyages beginning with one by Frobisher in 1576 vainly sought to find a 'North-West Passage' round the Americas to Asia. In 1594 a great Dutch navigator, Barents, set off in the opposite direction, following the earlier English explorers of the north-east. On his third attempt to find a way east through the Arctic, three years later, he died in the remote wastes of Novaya Zemlya. (In fact no one was to make a successful North-West Passage by ship until 1905, and the first complete north-eastern voyage to Asia was made in 1879.)

The early explorers put up with great hardships and showed great courage. But sometimes their enterprise and daring showed themselves in ways less admirable. One was their willingness to use force to gain commercial ends. In the end this tapered off into straight piracy, and by the time of Drake and the English 'sea-dogs' fighting about trade was already taken for granted in the Atlantic as it had been by Catalans and Genoese in the eastern Mediterranean.

An age of traders

Trading may well be older than civilization itself; certainly, since civilization began, there have always been traders. For a long time after the collapse of the Roman empire not much trading went on in western Europe except on a very local basis, and even that was probably mainly by barter. But this began to change with the revival of town life from about 1100 onwards. By 1500 Europe was swarming with merchants, still only doing very local business; they were even more numerous by 1800 and by then the scope of their operations was much bigger; it was, in fact, often world-wide.

The earliest great trading cities in the West had been Italian; Venice and Genoa had all but monopolized trade with the Near East, but other towns like Pisa and Florence were trading with one another, with Sicily and with the great north European fairs as early as the twelfth century. In the north the German Hansa towns of the Baltic were already involved in trade with Russia and Scandinavia in the Middle Ages. In the sixteenth century such pioneering centres were overtaken in prosperity by Antwerp. That port was a great shipping and manufacturing centre, through which wool from England and grain, fish and timber from the Baltic reached the growing populations of the Netherlands, Flanders and Picardy (the last two of which were important textile centres needing imported wool). Yet because of foreign competition and Spanish rule, Antwerp declined. Amsterdam succeeded to the domination of European trade and finance in the seventeenth century. Finally, after 1688, came the turn of the City of London.

These cities – and many others only slightly less famous – brought together the threads of a network of trade steadily growing more complicated and more extensive. Well before 1500 Venice, Genoa and the cities of Catalonia had linked Europe to the sea and caravan trade of Asia, the Indian ocean and the Persian Gulf, most of which flowed to Constantinople in the first place. Some of this business fell off after the disappearance of the Byzantine empire,

By the end of the sixteenth century London was England's busiest port. This view shows the river below London Bridge, with the Tower of London just right of centre on the far bank. No big ships could pass up stream beyond the Pool.

Quentin Massys's painting of a banker or money-lender and his wife in 1514.

but soon the North African coast began to provide new products, demands and markets.

Nevertheless the main expansion in trade for a long time took place inside Europe. The great traditional fairs continued to be important in channelling commerce into well-worn routes. But sea-borne trade steadily grew; it was cheaper than land transport. The first people really to exploit this were the Dutch, partly because of their position, partly because they had to earn money by trade in order to survive, partly because they had large numbers of seamen trained in the North Sea fishing fleets, and partly because they invented a remarkably efficient cargo-carrying ship, the 'flute' or 'fly-boat', which could carry a great deal and be managed by a small crew. Dutch commercial prosperity, which reached its peak in the seventeenth century, was based in the first place on bringing Baltic produce to western Europe, and on the selling of the marvellous salted and pickled herrings, still one of the delights of Holland.

All the earliest developments in the actual machinery by which business was done – the first banks, stock exchanges and devices like 'letters of credit', or 'discounted bills' which made it possible to make payments at a dis-

tance without actually carting bags of gold and silver about – were at first confined to trade inside Europe. A bank is basically a business which borrows money from some people in order to lend it to others. One of the reasons why families at first well known as money-lenders turned gradually into the first international bankers was that kings found it convenient to use them to pay armies operating abroad, or to transfer loans raised in one country for use in another. The business of paying, supplying and moving Spanish armies about in the sixteenth century, when they were operating over much of Italy, Lorraine and the Netherlands, created lots of business for financiers and merchants and required complicated networks of agents and offices. It was also important in the rise of international business that Spain – that is, Spanish America – was the source of a flood of silver which began to arrive in the sixteenth century. In the 1540s a vast silver mine was found at Potosi in Peru, which was so important that from it can be dated an abundance of bullion (America was to be Europe's main supply of currency until the nineteenth century) which both encouraged business (there was more money about) and gave people the first explanation to come to hand of an experience forgotten since the later centuries of the Roman empire: inflation.

Nowadays scholars are much less willing to be dogmatic about explaining the rise in European prices during the sixteenth century of something like 400 per cent. Given modern rates of inflation, this does not seem very shocking. But at the time it seemed awful and attracted much attention. Food prices were especially affected and it seems that real wages – that is, the standard of living – of the ordinary working man fell. Whatever the cause, the inflation had important results, one of which was to encourage trade; the commercial atmosphere in the sixteenth century was 'buoyant', even if there were hard times, and there were profits to be made by shrewd investors.

The African slave-trade

Some of the biggest profits to be made in trade between 1500 and 1800 were made by selling human beings to other human beings – slaving, as it was called. There was nothing new about slavery, of course. It was the basis of economic life in the ancient world and, though the enslaving of fellow-Christians had more or less disappeared in Europe during the Middle Ages, the Islamic world rested on it. Arab slave-traders even supplied African slaves to markets from which they were sold to masters as far away as China. After 1500 Europeans went back into dealing in slaves and built up a huge business by tapping a new source of supply, the western coast of Africa.

1442 is as good a date as any for the beginning of the story. In that year a Portuguese officer who had captured some Moroccan prisoners was ordered by his prince to take them back to Africa. When he did so, he got a quantity of gold dust and ten blacks in exchange for them. This was the beginning of the European slave trade in Africans. A new source of bond-labour had been found and other Portuguese set out to tap it. They built forts along the West African coast to collect their black victims. Soon a steady trickle of Negroes began to arrive in Europe. But settlements in America turned this trickle into a huge flood.

Nobody planned that this should happen. The first black slaves arrived in America in 1502, when the Spanish governor of Haiti was given permission to take with him Negroes born as slaves in Spain. A few years later a Spanish priest devoted to the Indians, Bartolomé de las Casas, was so appalled by his countrymen's treatment of them that he suggested that the Spanish settlers in Haiti should each be allowed to import a dozen Negro slaves. There were not enough Spaniards to do the work and las Casas believed that Africans would stand the labour better than the Indians. This was to have a bitterly ironical outcome, for, as a result, a favourite of the Spanish king Charles I (later the emperor Charles V) was allowed to import 4000 Negroes a year to the Caribbean islands. This privilege was sold in due course to Genoese merchants

Left: a sixteenth-century Benin bronze plaque showing a Portuguese soldier.

Elmina Castle (left), the first European trading port on the West African coast, was built by the Portuguese in 1482. They were forced to surrender it in 1638 to the Dutch, who had founded Fort St Jago (right) in opposition. By the late eighteenth century there were something like forty trading posts concerned with slaving.

and thus the slave trade became international business. In this way, protection was given to Indians at enormous cost to some Africans (though the Africans who supplied their fellow-blacks to the traders often did well).

The slave-trade expanded hugely in the next century when it was found that many of the Caribbean islands could grow sugar, a crop best handled on a big scale, on large plantations requiring a great deal of labour. Europe was short of manpower to develop the New World; Africa could make up the deficiency. As it grew more profitable to supply slaves to the Americas, so others joined the Portuguese in gathering cargoes of Negroes on the African coast. The trade was soon well worth fighting over, and that is how the Elizabethan 'sea-dogs', English sailors who sought to break into the slaving monopoly, appeared on the scene. The Spanish, though, with no West African bases of their own, had to rely on others to supply them, and control of trade with their own possessions became, in consequence, a grave problem.

Soon several Caribbean islands had acquired big black populations. By comparison the mainland Spanish possessions did not import many slaves (though the Portuguese took many to their colony in Brazil, with the result that there is an important Negro element in that country's population today). A Dutch ship sold some Negroes to British colonists in Virginia as early as 1619. This was a tobacco-growing area, where slave-labour was useful. Later the cotton and rice plantations of the Carolinas also began to use Negro slaves. From that time the mainland North Americans built up both a market and a trade to supply it and they grew steadily until the late eighteenth century. By then, there were something like forty trading posts on the West African coast concerned with slaving; Dutch, British, Portuguese, French and Danish.

When the trade was at its height in the eighteenth century, there were some years in which as many as 100,000 blacks were taken across the Atlantic, though exact numbers will never be known. But many more blacks left Africa than arrived in the Americas. They were packed closely into the ill-ventilated holds of ships, shackled so that they could hardly move, given a minimum of food and attention, locked in the dark for weeks on end. It is hardly surprising that disease, despair and brutality killed many – sometimes half a ship's cargo – before arrival in the New World.

The need for large numbers of labourers to work on the sugar plantations in Jamaica and other Caribbean islands was important as an encouragement to the import of slaves.

Sea-power and world trade

The slave-trade was only part of the story of new patterns of trade spanning the oceans, which were one major result of the age of discoveries. The result was a new world commercial system much more widespread than any earlier one. It was the greatest change ever made in the history of European commerce and by 1700 it was irreversible. Overall expansion went on faster than ever (though there were a few hiccups as things went wrong in particular places), and Europe's trade with the non-European world steadily loomed larger and larger.

Of this trans-oceanic commerce, the Atlantic trade with European colonies and possessions in America was the most important part. Ships would set out from the Atlantic European ports with trading goods. They would use them to buy slaves on the African coast. After taking them to the Caribbean and selling them – those slaves who had survived, that is – they would load sugar or coffee and take it back to Europe or the British North American settlements. From the latter, other goods – rum, indigo, rice, corn – would be exported to Europe or to the Caribbean colonies. The

Spanish, like the English and French, tried to reserve trade with their own possessions to themselves, though unsuccessfully, because of the huge profit to be made by smugglers and 'interlopers'.

The long-term victors in the struggle for the profits of world trade were the English. One reason was that the government in London was more single-minded in upholding the interests of English (and, after 1707, Scottish) merchants and sea-captains than were the kings of France in looking after those of their subjects. From Versailles (where the French court was based from the days of Louis XIV onwards) the view towards Europe always seemed more interesting than that out to sea; French kings were more concerned about conquest (or at least holding their own) in Europe than with fishing for cod off Newfoundland, selling slaves to the West Indies, or importing sugar and coffee. The greater British awareness of what these things might mean in terms of profit was one of the facts which helps to explain the rise of the Royal Navy to such commanding importance in world politics.

Politics and commerce were all the time becoming more and more mixed up. Sea-power did not just guarantee that you could get to other parts of the world and settle colonies there; it could also be used, as was British sea-power in the early eighteenth century, to force open the legal door to the Spanish colonial markets (illegal entry had already been won by the free-booters and pirates of the previous century, the great age of smuggling and buccaneering). Sea-power was also essential – especially in wartime – if your own traders were to be protected. It could also be used to back up diplomacy in negotiating favourable terms over, for example, customs duties levied

NORTH AMERICA / tobacco cotton / sugar rum / WEST INDIES / cloth iron goods / firearms brandy / WEST AFRICA / slaves / SOUTH AMERICA / 0 3000km

by a country on imports. Such things perhaps mattered more to Great Britain than to any other power, because she gradually emerged as the country which more than any other depended on overseas trade in order to earn money. The most valuable part of this trade was not the export of her own products, but the importing of colonial goods for resale in Europe or in the colonies.

In the world picture the trade with Asia, though the most glamorous, was far from being the most important in terms of bulk or value. Nonetheless it offered great profits to individuals and drew merchants like a magnet. Both the Dutch and the British established 'East India' Companies early in the seventeenth century with monopoly rights to trade in the Far East, and the French later followed suit. They became the main ways of contesting for trade in Asia, but they suffered from the disadvantage that, except for a few mechanical novelties, there was very little made by Europeans which the Asians wanted. With India, China and Indonesia the European countries therefore usually had what is called an 'adverse' balance of trade; they could not sell the Asians enough European goods to pay for what they

A Dutch couple, shaded by a servant, watch the fleet of the Dutch East India Company from a hill near Batavia (now Djakarta in Indonesia).

bought, and so had to pay for it in silver. It was another example of how, without anyone really intending it, the world was getting more tied together; the Spanish brought silver from the New World to Europe, where it paid the debts of the Spanish monarchy to bankers who then passed it on to merchants to use to buy goods in Asia. On the miners of America rested the financing of trade in Canton.

This is, of course, only a tiny part of the whole truth. The main lines of what was happening in these three centuries, though, are fairly clear. World trade was growing; the first part of it to grow really fast was the Atlantic trade; it became more and more tied up with politics and sea-power; and – above all – it was dominated by the Europeans. No Chinese junk or Arab dhow ever docked at a European or American port in these centuries, though thousands of European and American ships went to the Moluccas, India, the Persian Gulf and China. Even the Japanese let in a tiny trickle of Dutch traders to one of their ports.

European settlement overseas

It was not only trade that drew Europeans overseas. Some also went to live there. A few Vikings in the ninth and tenth centuries had been the first European overseas settlers – emigrants who actually intended to remain in foreign parts, making a living and establishing new communities there. The settlement of Iceland was their main achievement and a few also survived for a time in Greenland and, possibly, the North American mainland. No one followed them westwards until a few Portuguese and Spanish went to the Azores, Madeira and the Canaries in the fifteenth century. But the real story of the European creation of new nations overseas only begins a hundred years later in the Americas. It then unrolled so fast that by 1800 millions of people of European descent lived on the other side of the Atlantic. What is more, millions of non-Europeans had grown used to European government and civilization too.

The new European communities in the Americas formed three main blocs. South of the Rio Grande and over much of the Caribbean future nations were founded by Portuguese and Spanish settlers. (This was the area later to be called 'Latin America' – a name which seems to have been invented by a nineteenth-century French emperor, Napoleon III.) North of the Rio Grande lived settlers drawn from many other European peoples, though most of them were English-speaking. Finally, farther north still, along the St Lawrence river in Canada, was a smaller but very distinctive block of French-speakers.

That story had begun in the south. In 1499 Spaniards first penetrated the mainland in the area of what was later called Venezuela. A few years later, when Balboa's men crossed the isthmus of Panama in 1513, some of them settled down, built huts and sowed crops, a sign that they were there to stay. The European age on the American mainland had begun and by then there were settlers in many of the Caribbean islands too. The Americas grew more and more attractive to poor, land-hungry Spanish squires and soldiers of fortune as more became known about them.

From such men were drawn those whom the Spanish called the *conquistadores* – the 'conquerors'. The most famous of these half-heroic, half-piratical figures was a Spanish officer called Hernán Cortés. In 1518 he left Cuba for Mexico, burnt his boats on landing there, founded the town of Vera Cruz and then led his men inland to the high plateau which was the heart of the Aztec empire. Within a few months he had conquered it. A few years later, in 1531, another Spaniard, Pizarro (if possible an even more ruthless adventurer than Cortés), marched through the Andes to the Inca capital and destroyed the Inca regime. Thus Mexico and Peru both passed to the Spanish crown; the legends about them and their fabulous wealth which filtered home to Spain drew more Spaniards like a magnet to the 'Indies'.

The motives of those who came were very mixed. They wondered at the wealth of the native civilizations, and were excited by the possibilities of carrying off their treasures. For a long time men were to explore South America tirelessly, looking for the legendary city the Spanish called *El Dorado* – the golden place – because of its fabulous wealth. The *conquistadores* had gone to the mainland to look not only for gold, though, but for more land and for slaves to work the ranches and farms they had already built up in the islands. This was not likely to make them gentle to the Indians. Though they might sometimes wish to bring to the Indians the Gospel of Christ, they had

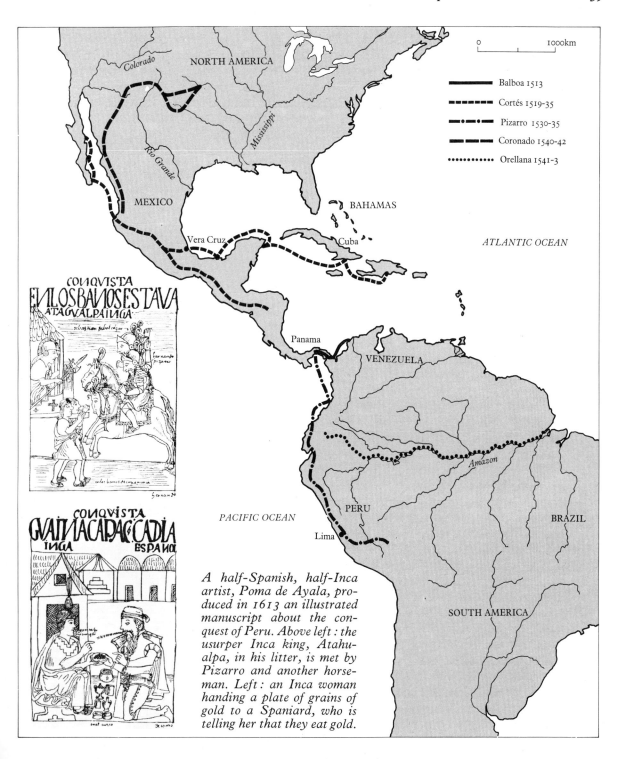

NORTH AMERICA

Colorado

MEXICO

Rio Grande

Mississippi

Vera Cruz

BAHAMAS

Cuba

ATLANTIC OCEAN

Panama

VENEZUELA

PACIFIC OCEAN

Amazon

PERU

Lima

BRAZIL

SOUTH AMERICA

0   1000km

━━━━━━ Balboa 1513
▬ ▬ ▬ ▬ Cortés 1519-35
▬·▬·▬· Pizarro 1530-35
▬ ▬ ▬ Coronado 1540-42
•••••••• Orellana 1541-3

CONQVISTA
E.LOSBAÑOSESTAVA
ATAGVALPAINGA

CONQVISTA
GVAINACAPAC CADIA
INGA   ESPAÑOL

A half-Spanish, half-Inca artist, Poma de Ayala, produced in 1613 an illustrated manuscript about the conquest of Peru. Above left: the usurper Inca king, Atahualpa, in his litter, is met by Pizarro and another horseman. Left: an Inca woman handing a plate of grains of gold to a Spaniard, who is telling her that they eat gold.

the militant Christianity which had won back Spain from the Moors in the 'Reconquest' behind them too, and they seem to have been genuinely horrified at such practices as the Aztec human sacrifices (though why men used to the idea of burning heretics should have been so offended by them is now rather hard to see).

The effect on the native populations of the arrival of the Spanish was almost uniformly disastrous. This was not entirely the fault of the new arrivals (unless it is argued that they should not have gone to America at all). The diseases they brought with them (smallpox was the worst) had a catastrophic effect, first in the islands and then on the mainland. It was possibly reinforced by the psychological shock of the Spaniards' power and seeming irresistibility; the Aztecs had never seen horses and could not at first believe their eyes when they saw men dismounting from the sixteen Cortés had brought with him, for they seemed to be watching beasts dividing themselves in two. The population declined rapidly (and this was the main reason why black slaves were soon needed in the islands; the labour supply there was soon too small for the settlers). A ruthless exploitation of native labour had followed Spanish settlement. After a little time churchmen began to fight against this, but they could not do much for the Indians. The usual arrangement was somewhat like a serf system, whereby a Spanish settler received the labour services of a native community in return for protection. As disease and overwork took their toll, it became all the more important to royal officials and settlers alike to prevent labourers from leaving the plantations where they worked and so the system was tightened up even more (rather as a shortage of labour caused the tightening-up of serfdom in eastern Europe from the seventeenth century onwards). One relic of this state of affairs is that over large areas of South America even today the word familiarly used for a peasant is *péon* –

the Spanish word for a pawn in a game of chess, the lowest-valued piece on the board.

The population slowly rebuilt itself by natural increase and immigration from Europe over the next two centuries or so and this led to societies in which an upper and middle class of mainly European blood ruled over large numbers of South Americans who

An illustration from a sixteenth-century Spanish manuscript shows mournful Mexicans, laden with their possessions, fleeing from the conquistadores, who can be seen approaching on horseback in the background.

In the 1590s the Protestant de Bry published an illustrated book, which did much to open the eyes of Europeans to the cruelties inflicted on the Indians by the Spaniards. The greed of the con-quistadores is contrasted here with Spanish religious fervour: the soldiers are quarrelling among themselves about their tribute of gold from the natives, while the priest carries on baptizing other Indians.

were predominantly Indian. Although neither the Spanish nor Portuguese much minded inter-marriage (the Spanish had long lived in a multi-racial society), the more European blood you had in colonial society, the more likely you were to be fairly well off and in a position of power. The people of predominantly European blood born in the Americas (*Creoles* was the Spanish name for them) were the rulers and landlords of the large Indian populations who were survivors of the old civilizations, almost all of whose spectacular past achievements disappeared. Many Indians came to speak a kind of Spanish and became Christian at least in name. This was the pattern over most of Spanish America.

The story was much the same in Portuguese Brazil, except that there was little in that country in the way of civilization to be displaced as there had been in Mexico and Peru. Moreover so many African slaves were brought there that the black cultural heritage of Africa was to be as important there as the Indian. As in the Spanish colonies, so in Brazil Christianity was one of the ways in which European civilization was most obviously and deeply implanted in a non-European setting. Other European imports were forms of government based on laws, traditions and institutions which went back deep into the European past and had no logical connection with American

society at all. So, after the empires passed away, a system of states on European lines, with civil servants and law courts like those of Europe, was to survive in South America.

The Spanish and Portuguese American empires were huge, even though for a long time there were only small numbers of European immigrants to exploit them. By 1700 the Spanish in theory governed an area running from the River Plate in the south to what is now New Mexico in the north. It included almost the whole length of the Pacific coast from southern Chile to lower California and its claims northwards stretched into what were to become Florida, Texas, New Mexico and California. These lands north of the Rio Grande were very sparsely inhabited even in 1800; over most of them there was no Spanish presence except a few mission stations and a fort or two, though they were to be the sites of cities very important in later times. 'New Spain' (as Mexico was called), Peru and some of the larger Caribbean islands were by 1800 much more thickly settled. The 'Indies' were governed in theory as sister kingdoms of Castile and Aragon by viceroys at Lima and Mexico, but in practice they had to be run with a fair degree of independence. Yet they were part of a world-wide empire, for by way of Acapulco and Panama, Spain was linked with the Philippine islands.

For a long time European colonies in North America looked very much less impressive than this. But by 1700 the eastern seaboard of the continent was divided into twelve English colonies. One of them, Virginia (named after Queen Elizabeth I, because she did not marry), had been the site of the first unsuccessful attempts to 'plant' a colony in the 1580s (early colonies were often spoken of as 'plantations'). Further attempts followed early in the next century but by the 1620s English settlers in the West Indies had achieved much more success than their cousins on the mainland. For a long time the North American colonies ran a poor second in economic attractiveness to what was going on in the Caribbean.

The seventeenth century finally brought efforts to settle in North America on a scale sufficient for success, and progress speeded up. By 1700 about 400,000 people of imported stocks (mainly British) lived in North America. The first settlement to survive had been set up at Jamestown, in the modern state of Virginia, in 1607; this was just a year before a French explorer, Champlain, built a small fort at Quebec, and only a few before Dutch settlements appeared on what is now the site of New York City. There was plenty of land in North America which could be cultivated on European lines, and the English began the practice of transplanting whole communities – men, women and children – who set to work on the land and raised crops. This made them independent of the mother country for many essential supplies. The next thing was the discovery that tobacco-raising – first in Virginia – provided a trading product for export. Tobacco was all-important in the early history of Virginia and that of the later colony of Maryland too; it was even used instead of money for accounting debts. It was the first of several 'staple' products – cotton, rice, indigo were to join the list – which gave the colonists the wherewithal to buy things they wanted from the mother-country. Canada never had such

a product, and this is one reason why French settlement grew only very slowly. When Louis XIV assumed his kingly powers in 1661, there were only about three thousand French people in Canada.

This de Bry engraving copied from an illustrated report by the English explorer, John White, shows the everyday activities of the Indians in the village of Secoton in Virginia. They made three plantings of corn a year in order to stagger the harvests. The new corn can be seen just behind the posts on the right. The green corn is behind it, and beyond that is the ripe corn, in a field guarded by a watchman. A religious ceremony is being carried out in the foreground while hunting for food goes on in the background.

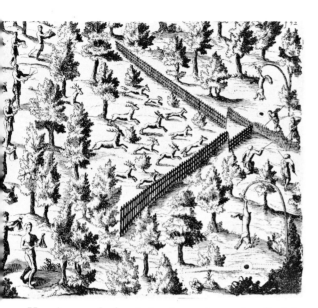

Hunting methods of the Iroquois as described by Samuel Champlain. By yelling and making loud noises, the Indians would drive the animals into the specially built stockades, behind which waited the armed hunters. Baited traps were also used (right) for catching individual animals.

Many of the English colonies developed from the first on distinctive lines. One explanation lay in different climatic and geographical conditions. Another was that 'New England' (as the northernmost group of colonies were soon called) began to attract men and women with strong and special religious views. They often held the more extreme Protestant doctrines of the Calvinists; they usually had very rigorous ideas about behaviour and disliked much ceremony in religious worship. They were not, on the whole, a very jolly lot; some of them became very irritated when an immigrant not so strait-laced as they actually set up a maypole. In England such people were called 'Puritans', and though many of them still thought of themselves as members of the Church of England when they came to America, they tended to break away from it when they had three thousand miles of Atlantic between them and home.

New England, in particular, became known as a place to which people came who wished to make more of a break with the old ways, while others went to the colonies farther south, like Virginia and the Carolinas. The most famous Puritan settlers – though nothing much was to be heard of them until the nineteenth century – were those who landed in 1620 from the *Mayflower*, the 'Pilgrim Fathers' who founded a colony at Plymouth, Massachusetts. With extreme views in religion also went a strong liking for self-government. This did not necessarily mean democracy. In Massachusetts government tended to fall into the hands of a very narrow circle of the well-to-do and the Calvinistic clergy, but in other colonies – Connecticut, for example, or Rhode Island – more democratic forms of government appeared.

None of the North American colonists had to deal with anything like the complicated, rich native societies of Mexico and Peru. North American 'Indians' in the seventeenth century were often only just entering the agricultural phase of their existence; their technology was neolithic. Nonetheless even this enabled them to offer valuable advice to the white settlers. In the early days those in Massachusetts were actually saved from starving by food provided for them by Indians. Unhappily this did not mean that the Europeans really treated them any better in the long run. Gradually the white settlements encroached on Indian hunting lands. There began a long-drawn-out era of conflict which was to end with the virtual extinction of many Indian peoples and the rest being driven into the west. This was one of the costs of increasing the opportunities which English America more and more obviously offered to thousands of poor Europeans. Drawn by its attractions, Germans, Huguenots and Swiss began to arrive at the end of the seventeenth century; the Dutch were already there. North America was by then already beginning to prove a 'melting-pot' of different stocks.

Oceanic politics

'World' wars took place even in ancient times, and raged over whole civilizations. Yet they were small beer by comparison with wars fought between 1500 and 1800. These were the first true 'world' wars in the sense that fighting took place all over the globe, and often over issues at stake thousands of miles away. This was another new feature of this age: it was the beginning of a period (lasting down to 1917 at least) when the way Europeans settled their own quarrels also settled willy-nilly the fate of millions of black, brown and yellow men who had never heard of Paris or London.

Some of the reasons for this will already have become clear. The growing European command of the sea, European economic activity all round the globe, the technological advantages Europeans increasingly enjoyed over non-Europeans all contributed to it. Another explanation, though, was that Europeans invented a new kind of empire, the oceanic empire, which depended on sea-communications. The acquisition of territory on the other side of the oceans was quite new and led irresistibly to quarrels between European predator nations right round the globe.

The origins of these quarrels lay for the most part in the growth of the new world-trading system. As a French minister put it to Louis XIV, 'trade is the cause of a perpetual contest in war and in peace between the nations of Europe'. So, for roughly two centuries, Spain, Portugal, the United Provinces, England and France sent out ships and built forts in order to try to keep to themselves trade with their own possessions or with local peoples with whom they were the first Europeans to begin to trade. These were the countries with coastlines which gave them destinies different from those of land-locked central Europe or the Mediterranean basin. Though the New World of the Americas was the main scene of their struggles, it was not the only one.

The first into the business of overseas empire had been the Portuguese and Spanish. Without consulting anyone else (though the pope afterwards said it was all right for them to annex any land not already belonging to a Christian prince), they agreed to divide between them any new lands which might be found anywhere in the world. One treaty, in 1494, said that everything west of a north-south line 370 leagues west of the Azores should be Spanish and everything east of it Portuguese (this is how Brazil, which falls east of the line, became Portuguese and was the only part of South America to do so); and another, in 1529, drew a similar line 297.5 leagues east of the Portuguese Moluccan islands. (A 'league' was usually about five kilometres.) This gave everything on the Pacific side of the line to Spain, everything west of it to the Portuguese (except the Philippine islands, kept by the Spanish). Roughly, this meant that the New World of the Americas was the Spanish sphere, and Africa, the Indian ocean and the Spice islands were Portuguese.

The spheres reflected in a measure two different kinds of imperial expansion. America, important though trade with it was, and interested in its exotic products though people became, was from the first a continent where Europeans *settled*; the Portuguese sphere of empire, on the other hand, was for the most part not one of settlement but of *trade*.

This stayed true for a long time: Europeans went to the Americas in growing numbers for three centuries but few settled in Asia and Indonesia. Those who did were usually planters or long-term residents who nevertheless hoped one day to go home after making their fortune. Because of this difference, what

An eastern demarcation line be-
tween Portuguese and Spanish
territories shown on a map of the
Far East (above) made a little
before it was agreed in the treaty
of 1529. The lines decided on by
both treaties show the new areas
theoretically reserved to Spanish
and Portuguese rule respectively
(right).

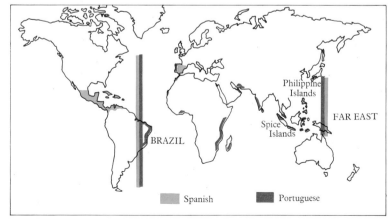

BRAZIL

Philippine
Islands

Spice
Islands

FAR EAST

Spanish   Portuguese

An example of the painted and dyed cottons (sometimes called 'Madras') which were such an important Indian export.

Right: a European tea-planter in India directs the work at his ease.

Europeans needed in the Far East (and on the African routes to the East) was not large tracts of territory but ports and stations – 'factories' was a favourite English word – where native traders could meet Europeans and business could be done. Often the native rulers gave permission for their creation and had to be respected; the shah of Persia, the emperor of China, or the Moghul emperor of India were the most powerful of them. European expansion in Asia in its early phases did not usually advance by conquest but by diplomacy and negotiation.

In the East the sixteenth century was dominated by the Portuguese, whose king consequently called himself by the splendid title of 'Lord of the Conquest, Navigation and Commerce of Ethiopia, Arabia, Persia and India'. South of Cape Verde they long had a virtual trading monopoly round to the Indian ocean and across it to the Spice islands. In 1517 they reached China and started direct trade between her and Europe, and forty years later they set themselves up ashore at Macao. They carried goods between Asian countries – Persian carpets to India, cloves from the Moluccas to China, Indian cloth to Siam – and won dominance over their Arab rivals from

bases at the entrance to the Red Sea and the Persian Gulf. All this rested on sea-power and careful diplomacy with native rulers, and it set a pattern for the next two centuries in the Indian ocean and Asia.

At the end of the century the Portuguese were elbowed aside by the Dutch, who set up an 'East India Company' in 1602 with the aim of replacing them in the spice trade to Europe – a rich prize. With ruthless skill they did so. Then, having pushed the Portuguese aside, they fought bitterly to keep the British out of trade in the Spice islands, and in the end were largely successful. By 1700 they had established a general supremacy over what is now Indonesia. Meanwhile the British for their part had installed themselves in a scatter of 'factories' round the coasts of India, from Gujarat to Calcutta. The Portuguese also kept some of their older stations in India, and the French and Danish had footholds there too.

Meanwhile relationships between European nations were being transformed by such enterprise. Not a word about non-European matters appeared in the peace treaties of 1648, but less than twenty years later, in 1667, the Treaty of Breda between England, the Dutch and the French was just as much concerned with

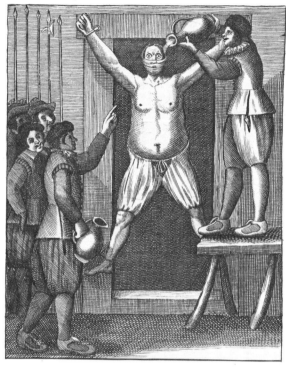

The struggle between the Dutch and the English for supremacy in the East Indies came to a head in the Amboyna massacre of 1623. English trading agents had been seized by the Dutch on false charges of conspiracy, and (with nine Japanese) were subsequently tortured and then executed.

affairs outside Europe as with those within. It ended the second of three naval wars between England and the United Provinces in which trade was the main issue; and seventy years farther on still, in 1739, two European nations, the United Kingdom and Spain, went to war over an entirely non-European matter. This was the first time such a thing had happened. It is a good landmark for the end of a period during which overseas questions had gradually come to loom as large in the eyes of diplomats as the more familiar European ones.

The war that began in 1739 has the attractive name of the 'War of Jenkins's Ear'. Nobody actually proved that the ear *did* belong to Captain Jenkins, but he produced it in a bottle of spirits before a committee of members of parliament and swore that it had been cut off by a Spanish coastguard in the Caribbean. Perhaps it had; anyway it was a plausible story. For decades English seamen had been trying to break into trade with the Spanish colonies and to take more of it than treaties entitled them to. For the same time the Spanish squadrons had been trying to catch them and had handled them roughly when they succeeded.

This was one side of a long struggle for a great prize, the right to sell goods to the inhabitants of the Spanish empire. The Spanish, who wanted to keep a monopoly of that trade for themselves, were always under the handicap of having to stick up for Habsburg policies in Europe and therefore of having to divide their forces. Spain could not abandon her colonial empire, because she depended on its revenues, but neither could she stop squandering its wealth on expensive involvements in Europe. The English were more favourably placed. They were involved in Europe, of course, but not so completely. And after 1707, when England was united with Scotland, they were truly an island people, safe from invasion across a land frontier.

The Anglo-French struggle for empire

Tangled up in the quarrels of England and Spain was another, longer-drawn-out contest between England and France. It began in 1688 when James II, the last Stuart king of England, was pushed off the throne in the 'Glorious Revolution'. 'Dutch William' (William of Orange) and his Stuart queen, Mary, then succeeded her father, and this brought England to the support of the Dutch (their bitter enemies only a few years before) against Louis XIV. There was much at stake overseas too, notably in the rivalry between English and French in North America. But the most important of the wars which followed was called the 'War of the Spanish Succession' because one of the greatest prizes at stake was the Spanish American empire, to which France had a claim when the Spanish king died without an heir in 1701. France was, like Spain,

handicapped by having to fight in Europe as well as at sea, where Louis XIV was at war with a coalition headed by the Habsburg monarchy. In 1713 the great peace of Utrecht, which ended the war, divided the Spanish inheritance: the Netherlands went to the Austrian Habsburgs, whereas a French prince was allowed to become king of Spain and its empire on condition that the Spanish crown was never united to that of France. By the same peace, the United Kingdom won big colonial gains, including many of the French Caribbean islands (she had started collecting from her

One of the most dramatic events of the 'wonderful year' (1759) of the Seven Years' War: General Wolfe's soldiers scale the Heights of Abraham and take the French stronghold of Quebec.

rivals there as early as the 1650s, when Cromwell's men had seized Jamaica from the Spanish) as well as a new, somewhat bleak but strategically important part of North America, Acadia, now renamed Nova Scotia (New Scotland). The British also won the right to trade with the Spanish colonies by sending one ship a year to Portobello – a concession to be used as a wedge to prise open the door farther and thus to lead in the end to the war of 1739.

That war soon involved France and Prussia, on the one hand, and Austria and Great Britain on the other. The British and French fought in India, where the French East India Company was by the 1740s hard at work dabbling in local politics in order to try and outwit its rivals and gain advantages. The French had also much expanded their area of influence in North America. During and after the War of the Spanish Succession, they had set up posts near the mouth of the Mississippi river, the entrance to the huge river system which dominates the centre of the continent. During the early eighteenth century expeditions had pushed up the river from the south, while others had made their way down it from the region of the Great Lakes. The result looked to the British colonists of the coastal plain more and more like a huge pincer operation, cutting them off from further expansion inland. In fact the French did not really settle the Mississippi valley and had no solid belt of territory inland. Nonetheless they built forts at strategic points (in this way future cities were founded, St Louis in 1682, Memphis the same year, Detroit in 1701 and New Orleans in 1718) and armed and encouraged the Indians against the British. It was clear that the French were not going to give up their claim to the interior without a struggle.

Fighting never stopped in India and America when peace was again officially made in Europe in 1748, and in 1756 yet another war broke out between France and England. Spain was only of secondary importance by now;

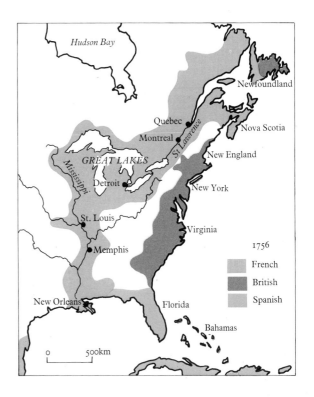

India and Canada were at stake. In this 'Seven Years' War' (peace was made in 1763) their fate was settled at the same time as that of the lands over which Prussia and Austria (now allies of the British and French respectively) were contending in Germany. The climax of the war came for Great Britain under a government dominated by William Pitt, who has a good claim to be the first British statesman wholly to grasp the possibilities of imperial power. He spoke of winning Canada in Germany, by getting his allies to pin down the French there, and he succeeded. At the peace, though it was less ferocious than some Englishmen hoped, Canada passed to Great Britain and India was made safe for the British East India Company. A string of British islands, added to by fresh acquisitions, all but enclosed the Caribbean, and within it there were British colonies in Jamaica, Honduras and the Belize coast.

Eastern Europe

Eastern Europe was a vast and shapeless region. Much of it had been for centuries a battleground between Teutonic and Slav peoples. It was pressed upon from the south by the Ottomans and (for a time) from the north by Swedish kings anxious to extend their lands south of the Baltic. Gradually, though, three things happened to give it a more established character. One was the firmer and further extension of serfdom in the northern plains of eastern Germany, Poland and Russia, and in the Danube valley. Another was the obliteration of such old medieval political landmarks as the Teutonic order of knights and the kingdoms of Poland and Hungary. The third was the emergence of three great powers, Prussia, Habsburg Austria and Russia.

Prussia was, in 1500, a small Baltic duchy under the lordship of the kings of Poland. A long line of soldier and administrator rulers built up its territories and power. They came from Brandenburg, one of the 'electorates' whose rulers voted in the election of a Holy Roman Emperor. Brandenburg's rulers took over Prussia in the sixteenth century and thereafter steadily added to their lands. They became famous for having the best army and civil servants in Europe. With their help, seventeenth-century rulers of Prussia turned back the Swedes, and an eighteenth-century king, famous as Frederick the Great, became the first challenger to the supremacy of the Habsburgs among the German princes. He opened a struggle with Austria which, though sometimes interrupted, was to last well into the next century.

Austria – or to be exact, the Habsburg monarchy – was the second of these great powers. The Habsburgs, challenged in Italy by the French, and then in Germany by France and Prussia in turn, gradually limited their ambitions more and more to central and eastern Europe. They made big gains from the decay of Poland and the decline of the Ottoman empire. But so did another power, whose emergence was the most important change of all in the east, Russia. By 1800 the strongest military power in Europe, so far as numbers went, her rise could hardly have been guessed at in 1500.

The core of the new empire was the old princely state of Muscovy. Its traditions stamped Russia with much of its character. The princes of Muscovy were autocrats and it was to be very important that Russian government was shaped by their ways rather than by, say, the more republican traditions of Novgorod. It was to Moscow, too, that the patriarchate or headship of the Orthodox Church had moved from Vladimir, its old location. The authority of that Church had been thrown behind the authority of the princes of Muscovy. Threatened by the Turks on the one hand and Roman Catholic German colonizers and Lithuanians on the other, the Orthodox Church after the fall of Constantinople had nowhere to look except to them.

In the fifteenth and sixteenth centuries the princes of Muscovy were very successful. In the middle of the fifteenth century their domains covered about 400,000 square kilometres. (They had been only a twentieth of that size in 1300.) In the 1550s they ran to nearly three million square kilometres, and by the end of the century Muscovy was as large as the rest of Christian Europe put together. Twice that area was then added in Siberia in the first half of the seventeenth century. There were still greater conquests to come.

This was an enormous transformation of the map, though for a long time it did not seem to affect the rest of Europe much: Russia was simply too far away and inaccessible and too little known. This was one reason why the princes of Muscovy so often got their way. Having been collectors of tribute for them in the Middle Ages, they were the obvious successors to the power of the Tatars when it began to ebb. Possible rivals – the Lithuanians and Teutonic Knights, above all – fought one another as well as attacking the Muscovites. Consequently, the princes of Muscovy were able to get on with the task of uniting all the peoples of Russia – the 'Great' Russians, the 'Little' Russians of the Ukraine, and the 'White' Russians of Belorussia – under their rule. The common tie of these peoples was religion and the language used by their priests, Church Slavonic.

Muscovy had other advantages too. The capital lay at the centre of Russian communications because it was at the focus of major river-systems. It was the main centre of Russian population from the fifteenth century on. To the immediate south lay the celebrated 'Black Earth' zone, the richest agricultural land in the country. It was from this base that expansion pushed outwards after 1462, when an outstanding ruler, Ivan III, came to the throne. He conquered Novgorod, expelling its merchant families and the Germans of the Hansa – and this meant the acquisition of the whole of the vast spaces of northern Russia. At times Ivan called himself 'tsar', a rendering of the old Latin 'caesar'; his grandson made 'tsar of all Russias' the title used until 1917.

Expansion continued under a succession of able (though occasionally mad) rulers. In nearly two hundred years (from 1389 to 1584) there were only five grand princes, a fact which goes a long way to explaining Muscovy's success. In 1682 there came to the throne another exceptional ruler, a man determined to modernize and extend his empire still further, Peter the Great.

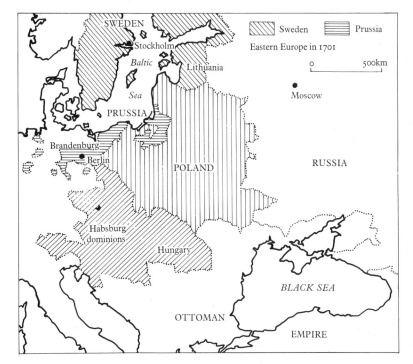

Before the building of St Petersburg in the eighteenth century, Moscow was Russia's capital. This view of it in 1573 shows the Kremlin, built inside the inner wall and overlooking the Moscva river on the left. Nearly all of Moscow's buildings were of wood.

Peter's greatest monument was the new city he founded on the Gulf of Finland, St Petersburg, capital from 1715 until 1918. This was his symbol of 'westernizing', of modernization, the process in which he was the first of many authoritarian reformers. To the political map too he brought great changes, giving Russia a firm grip on the Baltic coast and eliminating the threat from Sweden. Nevertheless, in altering Russian ways and life he had much less success than he hoped.

Russia was – and long remained – very conservative. For all the importance of trade in the great days of Kiev Rus and Novgorod, the merchant class was small. Towns were few. Most artisan trades were practised at a simple level by peasants rather than (as in the West) by specialists. Russia was overwhelmingly a peasant country. Of minor trading there was plenty, and there had to be because of the poverty of much of Russia's soil. But for a long time much of it was very local and rested on barter. Even when, as under Peter, deliberate attempts were made to encourage industrial enterprise, they did not change society as the coming of industry was to do in western Europe. Instead of throwing up a new 'middle' class of wealthy traders and manufacturers,

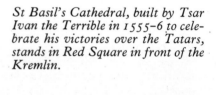

St Basil's Cathedral, built by Tsar Ivan the Terrible in 1555–6 to celebrate his victories over the Tatars, stands in Red Square in front of the Kremlin.

pursuing their own interests and standing between noble and peasant, industry was tied to the regime. It was the state which decided to open a mine, or set up a factory, not independent businessmen. This made Russia very different from western Europe.

Perhaps more striking still was the difference between the condition of the peasants in Russia and elsewhere. Even in eastern Europe, Russia stood out because of its dependence on serfdom. As 1800 approached, not only was the absolute number of serfs steadily increasing, but so was the proportion of the population which was serf (about two thirds of it by then). The legal powers of serf owners grew too.

One other great change in eastern Europe showed that Russia had established herself as a great European power. This was the obliteration of Poland. The 'Partitions' of Poland, as they are usually called, were carried out by her three neighbours, Prussia, the Habsburg empire and Russia, in three stages, in 1772, 1793 and 1795. At the end of them nothing was left of the once-great kingdom of Poland, and Russia had carried off over half the territory. She had also profited greatly from the retreat of the Ottoman empire and was by 1800 the dominant power in eastern Europe.

Left: as part of his westernization campaign, Peter the Great insisted that his boyars wore European clothes and went clean-shaven. (He personally cut off some of their beards.) Like changes insisted on by twentieth-century reformers in other countries such demands were symbolic of Peter's determination to remake his country's culture as well as its laws.

Right: Peter the Great's summer palace, built at the cost of the lives of many labourers on the marshes near St Petersburg. It was modelled on Versailles, but for many years before the Revolution it was not used by the Russian tsars, who preferred the less formal palace at Tsarskoe Selo, not far away.

The western Islamic world

For more than two centuries after the fall of Constantinople in 1453, large numbers of Europeans lived under Islam. Even more lived under its menace. Paradoxically, just as the long Reconquest of Spain had been completed, in the east Islam seemed more threatening than ever. This was partly an illusion, for Islam was divided; Persia was at times at war with both the Turks and the Moghul emperors of India, and Arab states contested Turkish power in the west. Still, the feelings of Europeans are comprehensible, for they were confronted with the sharpest of the cutting-edges of Islam, the armies of Ottoman Turkey.

In a series of naval offensives in the fifteenth and sixteenth centuries the Ottomans wrested many of her remaining possessions away from Venice – the Ionian islands at the mouth of the Adriatic in 1479, the islands of the Aegean in the 1550s and 1560s, Cyprus in 1571 – and forced the Spanish monarchy to fight hard to maintain its communications with Italy. Briefly the Turks even had a foothold there, while the posts captured by the Spanish on the North African coast early in the sixteenth century were quickly lost again as the Turks conquered Algeria, Cyrenaica, Tripoli, Tunisia one after another.

The Ottomans had by then over-run Serbia, Bosnia and Herzegovina in Europe itself. In 1526 they shattered the Hungarian army in a defeat so appalling that 'Mohács Field' is remembered still as a black day in the nation's history. Three years later they besieged Vienna for the first time, though unsuccessfully. In the early seventeenth century there was a pause in this advance but then it was resumed, Hungary being over-run for a second time (this was the last time the Turks overthrew a Christian kingdom), Podolia (the lower Ukraine) being taken from Poland, and Crete from the Venetians. Finally, Vienna was besieged for a second time in 1683. This was, at last, the highwater mark of Turkish power. From now on the Ottoman tide was to recede.

The Ottoman empire was not built only at the expense of Christians. In North Africa the Turks had established their overlordship over Moslems. By 1520 much of the Hejaz, Syria, upper Mesopotamia and Kurdistan were in Turkish hands. Suleiman the Magnificent, the great sultan who began to reign in that year, added to these conquests lower Mesopotamia, and much of Georgia and Armenia, and pushed farther into the Arabian peninsula too. By 1683 the Ottoman empire ran from the Straits of Gibraltar to the Persian Gulf and the Caspian, and it was to pick up more pieces of territory even after that date.

The divisions among the Turks' potential enemies in Europe was a great help. Until the end of the seventeenth century, in fact, no real danger threatened the Turks from Europe. Then the situation began to change rapidly. Broadly speaking, after the reign of Louis XIV, the main territorial questions of western Europe were settled and the boundaries of states there were to remain untroubled during the eighteenth century. But the appearance of two major new eastern monarchies – Prussia and Russia – altered very gravely the balance of power which faced Turkey. The Habsburgs, it is true, continued to be preoccupied in Germany and the West. It is also true that carving up Poland absorbed some Russian energies. Nevertheless Ottoman power had begun to roll back before the Austrians and Russians even before 1700. Hungary was recovered by then. Much worse was to follow, especially an important symbolic retreat in 1774, when overlordship of the Crimean Tatars was won by the Russians – the first surrender the Turks had to make of power over a Moslem people. By 1800 the break-up of the Ottoman empire in Europe was well under way; the Russians had much of the Black Sea coast, their frontier lay along the Dniester, and the Austrians had advanced to the Danube. Yet the whole process of dissolution was to take a long time – until 1918 in fact. In the Middle East the problem of deciding how the formerly Turkish lands should be divided still has to be settled.

Why was the pressure of powerful neighbours so quickly fatal to the Ottomans? The explanation lies partly in internal weaknesses. In the first place, for all its huge extent on the map, Ottoman power varied very much in effectiveness from place to place. In Mesopotamia (almost always disputed with Persia) and Syria the desert Arabs were never really under control. There was no centralized administration worth the name; the Ottoman empire was in most places a matter of arrangements be-

tween the 'pasha' – the Sultan's officer – and local bigwigs about the way in which taxes could continue to be raised. This gave local figures much power. Pashas themselves sometimes became something like petty dynastic princes as time went by. As a result the empire could never fully mobilize the resources it had, nor rely on loyalties among its subjects to over-ride the many divisions between provinces, peoples and religions.

The Ottoman 'state' was deeply marked by its origins; it had been put together more or less haphazardly in order to fight a holy war against the infidels. Such organization as it had was basically military; it was meant to provide recruits and taxes to pay soldiers and did this by arrangements not unlike the 'feudal' tenures of western Europe. This structure had already become corrupt by the seventeenth century. The sultan's officers often padded out their rolls of men in order to draw pay for more than they could actually produce.

A seventeenth-century Janissary, a member of the crack corps of the Ottoman army. Recruited from Christian boys who had been kidnapped in childhood to be brought up as soldiers, they were loyal only to the sultan.

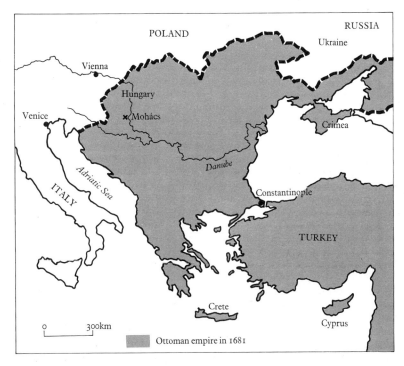

Ottoman empire in 1681

Locally they abused their position as recruiters and tax-gatherers. But there was no civil service to check them. The sultan himself was the centre of intrigue; favourites, the women of the harem, generals and religious leaders sought to influence him. The grand vizier, who held the major office of state, had to contend all the time with attempts to undermine his position. Outside the circle of the sultan, the nearest units to professional regiments which the Turks possessed were the Janissaries, once famous for their fighting but sadly decayed by 1700 and more of a nuisance and a danger to the sultan than a support; they frequently mutinied or went on strike over pay. Finally, throughout the Moslem community at large, real power was exercised by the religious leaders – the 'ulema' – whose attitude could determine popular support or discontent. This was very important. There were frequent tumults at Constantinople. After one

especially violent upheaval in 1730 the Bosphorus was said to have been covered for days by bobbing corpses.

Of modernization there was little. Almost all that was successfully achieved was the conversion of the navy in the 1690s from the old, oared galleys to sailing-ships of the European kind. But trained sailors were harder to get than galley-slaves had been (one sign of Ottoman decline during this period is the increasing employment of Europeans in the navy and army). Apart from this, there was virtually no attempt to learn from Europeans.

On one other front Ottoman power was slowly undermined. At the beginning of the sixteenth century a new dynasty of rulers had established itself in Persia, the Safavid family. It was of great importance that it belonged to the Shi'i sect – a seventh-century form of Islam which had long survived in opposition to the official 'Suni' version. Shi'i doctrines

In 1526 Suleiman the Magnificent conquered Hungary, which, as a result, accepted the overlordship of the Ottoman empire. The Hungarian king is being crowned by Suleiman (right); and Suleiman's successor, Selim II, is shown receiving a foreign taxpayer (below).

were almost always more widespread in Iraq and Persia than in Syria and there were many ramifications and sub-sects. They all rejected, though, the authority of the caliphs (their rulers). When the Safavid set themselves up in Persia therefore, they were almost bound to quarrel with their Ottoman caliph neighbours, who claimed the headship of Suni Moslems.

In 1514 Persia went to war with the Ottomans. For the next two centuries conflict with her was to prove a wearing distraction to them, forcing Turkey to fight on two fronts. Meanwhile the Safavid rulers – notably their outstanding shah, Abbas the Great – built up a new Persian empire, a centre of high civilization and wealth. At Abbas's death, it is said, his capital Isfahan was a great city with over 150 mosques and 300 public baths.

Yet the Safavid state was a harsh and intolerant one. It too had to fight on two fronts at times, against the Moghul emperors of India as well as the Suni Ottoman sultans. There were financial strains and the dynasty showed signs of degeneration. Occasionally the advocates of old-fashioned Shi'i austerity had some success in their complaints about declining standards; religious leaders had a spectacular success under a drink-loving shah at the end of the seventeenth century, when 60,000 bottles of wine from the royal cellars were publicly smashed. But small successes could not reverse the continuing tendency of the Safavids to go downhill. In 1722 the last of their line was overthrown by an Afghan warrior. A few more years of trouble followed until in 1736 a new strong man emerged, Nadir Shah. After expelling the Afghans, he took back provinces seized by the Ottomans and Russians, but this too was only an interlude. When Nadir was assassinated in 1747, Persia once more disintegrated and was only to recover in the twentieth century, under a new dynasty.

Two of the many mosques of Isfahan: the entrance to Sheikh Lotfullah Mosque, built for the harem of Shah Abbas (below) and Madreseh Madar Shah (right) built in 1694–1724 as a religious school, incorporating a mosque.

The decline of Moghul India

East of Turkey and Persia lay the other great Islamic power, Moghul India. Under Akbar (grandson of its founder, Babar) the Moghul empire was a powerful and magnificent state, though as a boy he had been forced to fight for his throne against other claimants (to one of whom he himself administered the fatal blow). The emperor himself was simply called 'The Great Moghul' by Englishmen who visited his court. Babar had quarrelled with his sons and was disappointed in them, but Akbar left behind a very solid and stable structure. His tolerant policy towards his Hindu subjects won their support and he married a Hindu princess. Meanwhile he conquered every native Indian kingdom within reach. By the time of his death in 1605, he had done so much to consolidate the position and prestige of his dynasty that it became fashionable among Indian princes and grandees to claim Moghul (that is, Mongol) descent. The only real problem of loyalty which Akbar faced was that of his Moslem followers, some of whom were outraged by his concessions to other religions and interference with strict Islamic practice.

Jahangir, Akbar's son, was a cruel, ruthless, drunken but cultured emperor who, like his own son and successor, Shah Jehan, extended the empire's boundaries still farther. It reached its greatest formal extent in the second half of the seventeenth century, in wars against the states of the Deccan which gave it a claim to the south, though most of this area was never really subdued. Shah Jehan's reign brought the peak of Moghul cultural achievement too, and from it comes the building which is possibly the best known of all monuments of Indian architecture, the beautiful Taj Mahal, which the emperor built as a tomb for his favourite wife. Some have thought it the peak of Moslem architecture in that it brought to perfection the traditional forms of dome and tall, slender towers.

It was only under the next Moghul emperor, Aurangzeb, who came to the throne in 1658, that signs of decline began to be obvious. It would not be true to say that decline actually started under Aurangzeb; already under Shah Jehan peasants were reported fleeing from the land and taking to banditry so as to escape the heavy taxation which paid for the Moghul wars in the south and against the Persians. (The court was expensive too: Shah Jehan had two underground strong-rooms at Agra, one for gold, one for silver, and each was over six metres square and nine metres high.) Nevertheless things took a quite decisive turn for the worse under Aurangzeb, when the tax-collectors seem to have made huge exactions. Furthermore, like his near-contemporary in Europe, Louis XIV, who persecuted his Protestant subjects, Aurangzeb seems to have been determined to tolerate no rival to the religion of his dynasty. He re-imposed the poll-tax on non-Moslems abolished by Akbar and discriminated against Hindus in government. The effect was to undermine the loyalty of non-Moslems which the regime had won under his predecessors. It also made it much harder to deal with the Mahratta princes of central and southern India – Hindu potentates who were a thorn in the side of the Moghul empire from this time onwards.

Their importance became clear after the death of Aurangzeb in 1707. Three of his sons immediately disputed the succession, and between 1712 and 1719 there were no fewer than five puppet emperors at Delhi. Combined with other weaknesses, this gave the Mahrattas their chance, and they took it so well that in the end they built up a confederation which stretched right across India from their capital at Satara, a little south of Bombay, almost to Calcutta in the east. As the empire bent under these strains, provincial governors – 'nawabs', as they were called – began to be more careless about their loyalty and looked to their own interest. The decay of the Moghul empire had begun.

The outcome might in any case have been fatal, but was probably made so more quickly because of Europeans. In the sixteenth century the Portuguese had dominated European trade with India. Though they were not treated with much concern by the Moghul authorities (they had first made contact with Hindu princes with whom they got on well), they soon showed they meant to stay. Goa, which they occupied in 1510, was the first Indian territory to be governed by Europeans since the days of Alexander the Great. From the start Portuguese rule encouraged mixed marriage (to begin with there were widows of Moslem soldiers killed by the Portuguese available as brides) and this has left its mark in many Indian family names to this day. Yet Portuguese power was already waning before the end of the sixteenth century. Perhaps this is why the Moghuls did not take much notice of other European arrivals during the reign of Akbar (and it was not until he had conquered Gujarat in the 1570s that Akbar had direct contact with the sea and the Portuguese). Under Jahangir the Portuguese fell out of favour because of their attacks on Moghul ships; the age of the English in India now began.

In 1639 the English were allowed to found Fort St George, a station on the east coast at Madras and the original base of their power in India. A few decades later they acquired other sites for trading posts – 'factories' – at Bombay, Calcutta and elsewhere, but none of this amounted to more than a few square miles. A rival appeared beside them when the French founded their East India Company in 1664. It too was to expand, and a century of

conflict between the English and the French followed. Rivalry was intensified after 1700, which was about the time when the London East India Company finally gave up hope of overcoming the ferocious opposition of the Dutch in the trade of Indonesia and the Spice islands and decided to concentrate on India. Then came the death of Aurangzeb. As the decline of the empire into anarchy accelerated, Englishmen began dabbling in the politics of Moghul versus Mahratta. They had also by then launched a revolution in English drinking habits by sending ships to China to fetch cargoes of tea for re-shipment; tea was to become the national drink of the United Kingdom and in the 1770s ten thousand tonnes of tea a year were leaving Canton.

The directors of the Company had for a long time been uninterested in acquiring territory; all they needed was a plot of ground on which to put up a warehouse and perhaps a few houses for their servants. They might even fortify

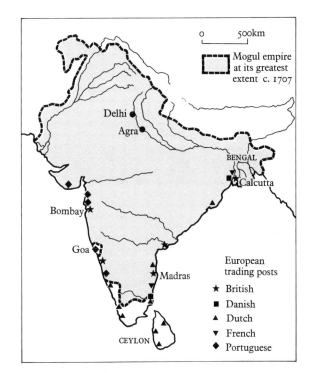

0	500km

☐ Mogul empire at its greatest extent c. 1707

Delhi
Agra

BENGAL

Calcutta

Bombay

Goa

Madras

European trading posts
★ British
■ Danish
▲ Dutch
▼ French
◆ Portuguese

CEYLON

these. But they were not out to paint the map red – to use a phrase coined much later. They were after trade, because that was where the profits lay, not involvement in government, which was expensive and time-consuming. On the whole their political interest in the decaying Moghul empire lay in securing the favours of local notables. These could in their turn use the support and assistance of the Company to strengthen their own position. This favoured British and French alike in the early eighteenth century, when the sub-continent in effect dissolved into a collection of more or less independent powers – the Mahratta princes of the Deccan, the Sikhs (a breakaway Hindu religious brotherhood which had turned to militant resistance to the Moghuls under Aurangzeb), and nawabs fishing in troubled waters for their own advantage. In addition to all these calamities, the empire was also faced from time to time by Persian invasions of the Punjab which it could not meet properly because of the Mahrattas to the south. In 1739 the Persians sacked Delhi and retired with Shah Jehan's famous peacock throne and the Koh-i-noor diamond (now among the British crown jewels).

Against this background it is perhaps sur-prising that the advance of the European Com-panies was as slow and as long-delayed as it was. In the 1740s, though, it began to gather speed when news reached India that England and France were at war. The British were in a specially favourable position. They usually

Top right: the Indian and Persian empires often fought over their frontiers. After a dream, when he saw himself being embraced by a submissive Shah Abbas of Persia, Jahangir commissioned this painting. It shows him as the greater of the two; they are standing on the globe with a lion and a lamb lying together (symbols of peace) at their feet.

Right: Shah Jehan seated on his peacock throne.

controlled the sea, and from their station at Calcutta they were well placed to step in when Bengal, the richest province of India, began to slip out of Moghul control. Peace in Europe in 1748 did not end armed conflict between the two Companies. The Seven Years' War was the decisive struggle. French interests in India were in the hands of an ambitious governor, Dupleix, but he was given inadequate support by the French government. The British were successful first in the south and Dupleix was recalled. A few years later they seized Bengal, after the nawab had committed himself against them (and had brought about the death of numerous British prisoners by locking them up for a night at the height of summer in the soon-notorious tiny 'Black Hole' of Calcutta). His defeat at the battle of Plassey in 1757 was truly one of the decisive engagements of world history (though not a very bloody one) because it sealed the fate of India for the next hundred and fifty years. It made possible the acquisition of Bengal, whose tax revenues could pay both for its government without cost to the Company and for the final destruction of French power in India. So began the story of British government in India – the 'Raj', as it was to be known.

The Moghul empire still existed in law, and the emperors still lived like ghosts at Delhi. But a new, successor empire was in the making, and it was one quite unlike any other European empire so far seen. For the first time a European state (and a very small one) acquired millions (later hundreds of millions) of new subjects without any intention of assimilating them to European ways, or of converting them to Christianity. India was to be as profoundly marked by the experience as was Great Britain, whose diplomacy, strategy and trade were to be increasingly affected by the weight of India inside her empire. That, of course, was also to shape world history, since Great Britain was to be the preponderant world and imperial power of the next century.

Akbar's tomb, near Agra, (above) and the Taj Mahal (below).

China's last age of isolation

Even in 1800 China looked remarkably remote, unapproachable and self-sufficient. A fifteenth-century Ming decree had forbidden Chinese ships to sail beyond coastal waters and individuals were not allowed to travel abroad. In 1525 officials were ordered to destroy all junks with two or more masts. There were to be no more expeditions to the African coast in big ocean-going junks and a run-down of the imperial navy began which was in the end to cost the empire dear. Meanwhile, though carefully supervised, Europeans had not been kept out altogether. Appetites long whetted by the accounts of medieval travellers such as Marco Polo, they arrived in growing numbers as the centuries passed. The first 'ocean devils' (as the Ming used to call Europeans) to secure a permanent settlement in China were the Portuguese, who, after a quarrelsome start which led to fighting, were allowed to establish themselves at Macao, near Canton, in 1557, where they have remained ever since. As time passed, though, the biggest single European community in China grew up at Canton, to which foreign trade was restricted in the eighteenth century. By 1800 there were about 1000 Europeans there, most of them merchants.

Missionaries had followed the Portuguese traders and adventurers and with some success. The Jesuits were particularly good at winning the confidence and interest of many of the scholar-officials. They threw themselves with enthusiasm into studying Chinese, often adopted Chinese dress, and made many concessions to Chinese ideas in the way they explained Christian doctrine to their hosts. In the end this was fatal; rumours reached Rome that some Jesuit fathers were going too far and were in danger of being paganized by their

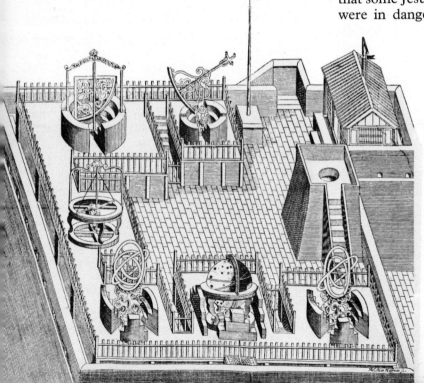

Left: the Jesuit observatory in Peking. The Jesuits managed to prove to the Chinese that their astronomers' methods of calculation were out of date, and in 1611 Jesuits were appointed the official court astronomers. Their success at regulating the calendar led to their being allowed to begin missionary work in China.

Right: a Dutch view of the Chinese in 1670. Because of their isolation, the Chinese were still considered by the West to be strange creatures with barbaric customs.

Chinese hosts. The Jesuits were therefore withdrawn at the end of the seventeenth century.

Before the Jesuits left, China had again acquired a new dynasty, the Ch'ing. Its Ming predecessors had shown the familiar symptoms of a loss of grip soon after 1500. They had lost control of outlying dependencies such as Tibet and Indo-China. Internal troubles had broken out in rebellions. Finally, in 1644, a Ming general asked for help from a non-Chinese people, originally nomadic, who lived north of the Great Wall. This was the old story of 'barbarians' being invited into the empire to serve Chinese ends, just as had happened many times before in the history of China (and, for that matter, the history of Rome too). These people were the Manchu, the last of a long succession of 'barbarian'

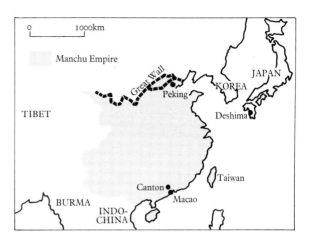

peoples of nomadic origin who, for two thousand years and more, had time and again broken into the history of the great centres of civilization round the huge perimeter of Asia. Their era of history was coming to a close; the Manchu were the last empire-building nomads.

Soon the Manchu struck out for themselves and put one of their own men on the imperial throne, and that was the end of the Ming. It took thirty years or so for Manchu rule to be established firmly all over the empire (the Dutch helped by supplying ships for the invasion of Taiwan). In spite of the fighting, it did not follow that there was a violent disruption of Chinese history. The country north of the Great Wall (which was not then called by its later name, Manchuria) had long been somewhat under the influence of Chinese civilization. Like many so-called barbarian peoples, the Manchu were by no means backward or primitive. They had been attracted by many features of the life and ways of a powerful and influential neighbour with a higher civilization. They had already begun to imitate some of those ways before their take-over of the Chinese empire. This meant that they were inclined to leave many things as they were and to try to restore the former glories of the 'Middle Kingdom'. What is more the

Manchu were a minority, never more than about two per cent of the whole population. The Manchu invasion therefore was another of those dynastic breaks in Chinese history which proved in the end not to change very much after all.

The most notable difference was that Manchu generals and officials took their places beside the old official class. This at first caused some envy and friction, but by and large government went on much as before. (The only visible difference for many people must have been the adoption by officials of the Manchu custom of wearing pigtails.) The greatest of Ch'ing emperors (as the Manchu dynasty was called), K'ang-hsi, though an admirer of European skills, carried his own respect for things Chinese to a remarkable degree, rebuilding Peking in traditional style and endowing research and scholarship in Chinese literature and history on an unprecedented scale. Though a quick-tempered man (he once went for two of his sons with a dagger), K'ang-hsi was prudent in conciliating his subjects and appointed Chinese generals and viceroys to high office. He was a hard-worker, who liked to keep a close eye on business, and lived simply when on his frequent campaigns. (He also turned 4000 eunuchs out of the palace, which must have been an economy.) Jesuits praised his 'nobility of soul' and it does not seem that they were simply flattering him.

He was a great restorer of Chinese power. He recovered control of Taiwan, reoccupied Tibet (it was to be lost again, though, a few

In 1793 a British mission, headed by Lord Macartney, arrived in Peking to ask the Chinese to lift trade restraints between the two countries. The Chinese treated Lord Macartney as if he were a vassal of the emperor, and even tried, unsuccessfully, to exact the ceremonial prostration or 'kowtow' from him. The emperor met him with a great show of ceremony but dismissed him (politely) without giving him what he asked for.

years later) and mastered the Mongols who had continued to harass the Ming; this was the end of the age-old nomad threat. Farther north Chinese troops in the Amur valley in 1695 attacked a post which had been set up by the Russians at a place called Albazin. They forced the Russians to withdraw and destroyed their fort. Thus the first round in a long and interrupted conflict with Russia – the only European power with which China shares a land frontier – went to the Manchu. Still, though the Russians might withdraw from the Amur valley, in due course they would be back. By 1700 they had in fact established themselves in Kamchatka. K'ang-hsi's successors also carried on the good work by reimposing Chinese overlordship on Korea, Indo-China and Burma, and the dynasty ruled a larger area than ever before. With strong land frontiers, the Ch'ing continued to neglect the sea, building no navy, but relying on coastal defences.

Meanwhile, though there was a long period of peace and prosperity at home (which accompanied another flowering of Chinese culture), this led to population growth and therefore (since China could not much increase her agricultural output with traditional methods) to more trouble for the future. By 1800 the pressure of numbers on food supply was again causing famine and peasant unrest. China (then with about 320 million inhabitants) had not, like Europe, succeeded in passing from a pattern of waves of population growth to one of a steadily rising curve.

Nor, for all the self-confidence they showed, were the Chinese preparing themselves in any way to face the future psychological and political threat from the 'ocean devils'. They believed that the empire already had all the materials and skills needed for civilization in its highest form and could gain nothing by closer contact with the remote nations of the globe.

Behind a seemingly invulnerable façade traditional ways went on remarkably undisturbed. Yet China's very assurance was in the end one of the worst obstacles to dealing effectively with the dangers threatening her from the white 'barbarians'. As long ago as Ming times the Chinese had allowed the technological and scientific superiority of their civilization to slip from them and this was to prove a grave handicap in the age of aggressive European expansion.

Two eighteenth-century Chinese engravings showing rice cultivation. Despite twice-yearly harvests possible in some regions, many Chinese lived near or at starvation level.

Japan goes her own way

Japan's culture owed much to China, and there were some important ways in which the two countries were similar, yet they responded to European influences very differently. As early as 1542 a Portuguese ship bound for China was wrecked on the Japanese coast. Some muskets were salvaged from her and expertly copied by the Japanese; soon these weapons were widespread and enthusiastically employed. For the first and certainly not for the last time, Japan happily borrowed something useful from Europe.

In Japan, as in China, the Portuguese were once more the pioneers of European enterprise. Their traders, who arrived in the 1540s, were soon followed by missionaries. Notable among them was the Jesuit St Francis Xavier (one of Loyola's original band) who landed in 1549. Large numbers of conversions soon followed; Christianity proved much more attractive to the Japanese than to the Chinese. In 1582 the Jesuits reported the existence of 200 churches and 150,000 Japanese Christians. Meanwhile, European traders had been given permission to set themselves up at Nagasaki, which was opened to foreign trade in 1571 by the local nobleman, who was a Christian.

The tide soon turned. An edict of 1587 banned Christianity and ordered all missionaries to leave. Many did, but the ban was not strictly imposed. Early in the seventeenth century, though, the authorities became alarmed at the continuing spread of Christianity. After expelling the Portuguese missionaries and banning further entries, they launched a ferocious persecution. Its climax came in a rising near Nagasaki by Christian Japanese in 1637 which culminated in a massacre of nearly 40,000 of them (a Dutch ship had helped to suppress the rebellion). A Portuguese embassy was slaughtered in 1640. Their compatriots, like English and Spanish merchants who had followed them to Japan, all left. Only the Dutch remained, with permission to have a small station on an island in Nagasaki harbour. They were obliged to show their respect to the local authorities by ceremonially trampling upon a Christian crucifix if required to do so. Embittered competitors used to say that a Dutch captain would sail to hell to trade with the devil himself were it not that his sails might catch fire.

This brought the progress of Christianity in Japan to a halt. The persecution was the work of a remarkable regime which had emerged in 1600. The anarchical struggles of great baronial families and feudal lords of earlier times had already been overcome by a great but lowly-born national leader, Hideyoshi. At his death in 1598 his vassals fought for power and one of them, Tokugawa Ieyasu, defeated his rivals. This was the beginning of the Tokugawa period and of the government called the bakufu – or 'government of the camp'.

The Tokugawa were one of the great noble families of Japan. The commander-in-chief of the imperial forces (the shogun) had often stepped forward in the past to rule in the emperor's name, sending him off to purely ceremonial duties while the real power was exercised in his name. After the great warrior Ieyasu became shogun in 1603, a succession of lords drawn from his family held the office for two centuries. The Tokugawa shoguns became hereditary princes, and the already great wealth and power of the clan grew even greater, thanks to their efforts and opportunities. It has been estimated that, by the middle of the seventeenth century, the Tokugawa owned about a quarter of Japan's rice-growing land and were the centre of a network of relationships binding the aristocracy to them.

A detail from a late-seventeenth-century map showing the port of Nagasaki on the left, with the Dutch enclosure, Deshima, protruding into the sea and joined to the main port by a bridge.

The Tokugawa shoguns ruled a society firmly organized in layers of distinct classes since the days of Hideyoshi. The top class were the samurai, warriors who were the retainers of the great lords – somewhat like European knights. Originally they had been given estates by their patrons in return for loyalty and military service but by the seventeenth century they lived idly in the castle town of their lord, paid a regular allowance in rice from his lands, with nothing really to do except attend him on ceremonial occasions. Below the samurai came peasants, artisans and merchants, the last regarded as the lowest in society because they were non-productive.

Japanese towns grew in size and importance. In 1800 Osaka had over 300,000 people and Yedo about a half million. Towns create new demands and markets. In the case of Japan they were one reason for the appearance of a flourishing trade in printed books and coloured woodblock prints. With books went ideas too, and at the end of the eighteenth century there were already a few signs that some Japanese were starting to wonder whether their isolation from Europe – a few books from Europe could be obtained through the Dutch – was not being purchased at too high a price. That isolation had been imposed at about the same time as the Tokugawa persecution of the Christians; Japanese were forbidden to go abroad, those abroad were not allowed to return and the building of large ships was stopped. Even the permitted trade with the Dutch was cut down in the eighteenth century. This cut Japan off from Asia as much as from Europe. It also helped to make Japan an even more distinctive country than in 1500. But, when change came to challenge it, Japan was to respond in ways very different from those of either India or China. Already in the eighteenth century the study and even the translation of European scientific books had begun.

Africa

Before 1500 the most important civilized peoples with whom Africans came in contact were Moslems. Except for Christian Ethiopia (and that was a pretty barbaric place) there was virtually no African contact with any other civilization except that represented by Portuguese slavers. But North Africa was dominated by Arab, Berber and Moroccan States, and for centuries they had been the source from which Islamic influence had been able to spread to the south. Traders, travellers and missionaries had penetrated Negro Africa in two main directions: up the Nile into the Sudan, and across the Sahara to the regions of the upper Niger and Senegal rivers. In addition there was another region of Islamic influence on the east coast. Zanz, as the Arabs called the coast, had been visited by Arab traders since pre-Islamic times, and Arab and African trade and intermarriage had produced a new language, Swahili, spoken over a large area. Thirty or forty seaports between Kilwa and Mogadishu sheltered a flourishing trade with Arabia, the Persian Gulf, India and, it seems, even China and Indonesia.

The huge area of Africa untouched by Islam is much more mysterious. In West Africa great kings had ruled large areas in the past, but by the sixteenth century not much remained of the empire of Ghana, and that of Mali was about to collapse. Over the rest of the continent societies were small in scale. Africans lived in groups which numbered at most thousands, though sometimes they were linked together under the vague overlordship of one ruler. For want of a more exact term, we

A Benin saltcellar carved in ivory and commissioned for a Portuguese monarch. Although clearly African in style, it shows the Portuguese influence in the figures of the soldiers round the base.

A typical seventeenth-century Dutch farm in Cape Town.

A stylized Ethiopian wall-painting of St George and the dragon.

have to call them 'tribal'. Each of them regulated affairs in its own fairly small territory according to its own customs and traditions, and many often claimed a common ancestor. For a living, these peoples practised agriculture at a fairly low level, herding where it was possible, but still sometimes hunting and gathering too. In West Africa some of them had a high degree of somewhat specialized metal-working skills; in East Africa there were others who knew a lot about mining.

This was Africa just as Europeans were beginning to develop their own first serious contact with it. Much of the continent remained like this for the next three and a half centuries, and it was not until the nineteenth that Europeans knew much more of it than a few coastal patches. As for European settlement, except at the Cape of Good Hope, where the Dutch established themselves in the middle of the seventeenth century, there was virtually none that mattered south of the Maghreb until the twentieth century.

Italian trading cities like Pisa and Genoa provided Europe's first peaceful and direct contact with North Africa in the Middle Ages. An occasional European had gone inland; in 1405 a Frenchman actually reached the Niger. The Portuguese and Spanish were soon afterwards extending their grasp of part of the Moroccan coast; something like a continuation of the Reconquest was under way there. But this was not to be the area of the first major European impact on Africa, which was to be made on the west coast farther south and was above all the work of the Portuguese. It took a long time to develop, and it was about a century before the Portuguese rounded the Cape of Good Hope. This was because of climate, the slowness with which knowledge could be built up and investment found for voyages, and the lack of good harbours and major river inlets. In retrospect, though, this seems a remarkably rapid performance. Soon others followed, though the Portuguese dominated the first age of African enterprise, with colonies well established in Angola and Mozambique before 1600. English ships began to visit the Guinea coast in the 1550s.

By then the slave-trade was in full swing. The profits which might be made from it had begun to outrun in attractiveness the original temptations to exploration – the wish to find a way round Islam to Asia, the search for the source of the mysterious gold brought back from Africa by the Arabs. There was, though, also a missionary interest; the Portuguese had some success in conversion among the peoples of the Congo basin. But it was slavery which came to dominate the West African trade.

African slavery was, of course, not new; Negroes had for centuries provided slave-labour for the Moslem world. It seems likely, though, that the impact of the Atlantic slave-trade greatly changed the lives of Africans in some regions. We know that in the interior it led to conflicts, as tribal rulers fought one another to win the prisoners they could sell to the Arab traders who took them to the coast. In the west such African conquerors were more likely to sell their victims direct to the European slave-traders who called there. In return it became quite usual to supply them with firearms and powder. In this way slavery was a disrupting force a long way from the coast and shaped the 'politics' – if that is the word – of Africans' relations with one another.

As for the drain on African populations it produced, that can hardly be accurately computed. We know that altogether, while the slave-trade lasted, something like nine or ten million black slaves were sent across the Atlantic. But what effect this had on population history is almost impossible to say. There may have been a balancing factor at work too, in that new food plants brought to Africa from America by the Portuguese in the sixteenth century – maize, sweet potatoes, cassava – made such a difference to African agriculture that the drain of slavery was offset by natural increase following on a bigger food supply. But this is only guesswork. And the Europeans, after all, brought other things with them, notably diseases to which Africans were terribly susceptible because they had been so long protected against them by their isolation. No one is likely to agree about the balance of the results of such forces. What is obvious enough is that their effects on Africans' lives could be enormous and in some places probably were.

In the interior, sheltered from regular incursions by Arabs or Europeans, African life must have gone on pretty much in the old way for centuries after 1500. So long as the gold in easily worked mines held out in East Africa, its peoples seem to have maintained a higher level of technological skill in building than other Africans, if the ruins of their greatest site, at what is now called Zimbabwe (the word simply means 'great house'), are anything to go by. By comparison with such monuments as Stonehenge or the Maya pyramids, they are not remarkable; but they are the peak of what sub-Saharan Africa is known to have produced without the aid of stimulus and technical knowledge from outside.

The only non-Moslem African nation with a literate culture was Ethiopia, so long insulated by Islam from contact with the remainder of Christendom that it was sometimes believed to be the kingdom of the legendary Christian prince 'Prester John'. In 1490 a Portuguese who reached the Ethiopian court carried a letter addressed to him. For a time it looked as if the Portuguese might prosper in Ethiopia, whose emperor asked them for help against the Moslems. Jesuit missionaries were at first welcomed there, but this welcome fizzled out. There were quarrels and the Jesuits were expelled in the seventeenth century. Ethiopia then resumed her isolation as the only Christian African kingdom. She was to be alone among African states too in remaining independent of European rule until well into the twentieth century.

The Portuguese first made contact with the African kingdom of Benin in the late fifteenth century. By the middle of the sixteenth century Portuguese trading 'factories' had been set up there. This seventeenth-century engraving shows the Oba (the Benin ruler) in procession.

Below: white exploration of tropical Africa was, until very recently, handicapped by the need to carry all equipment on the backs of native porters.

The dawn of the Pacific age

Nowadays we are all used to the idea that much of the interest of world politics has shifted from the Atlantic hemisphere, which dominated it for so long, to the Pacific (much as, earlier, it had shifted from the Mediterranean basin to the Atlantic). It is easy to see why. Around the Pacific are grouped not only the greatest powers of today, but some of the world's major industrial regions and greatest concentrations of population.

By 1800 its geography was pretty well known; the outline of the world's map had been completed. Magellan in 1521 had been the first European captain to cross the Pacific (he took over three months to get from Cape Horn to the Philippines) and this was only eight years after a European had first seen the ocean. In the seventeenth century came the discovery and mapping of much of the coast of Australia. Dutch explorers were already at it in the 1620s. Tasman, one of them, proved in the 1640s that Australia was not part of Antarctica (though he seems never actually to have sighted Australia while discovering Tasmania). He also touched New Zealand (pre-viously unknown) and discovered Tonga and Fiji.

In the eighteenth century the lead in Pacific exploration passed to other nations. Before 1700 William Dampier, an Englishman, had sailed along much of the western and north-western coasts of Australia. In 1739 a French naval officer, Bouvet, who had deliberately set out to settle whether a southern continent, such as that reported in legends, actually existed by sailing south until he came to one (or failed to), sighted land 2250 kilometres south of Cape Town. This was not yet within the Antarctic circle, but it revived the hope of finding such a continent, which would thus form a southern edge to the Pacific. Two other Frenchmen, Bougainville and La Pérouse, then added enormously to the detailed knowledge of the Pacific, north and south. Peter the Great had already sent off a Dane to explore the North; his name (Bering) is commemorated by the Strait named after him and he also discovered the Aleutian islands. Meanwhile a Russian had reached the eastern end of the Asian land-mass by sledge.

Left: members of the expedition of the great French explorer, La Pérouse, measuring and drawing the statues of Easter Island, unaware that the islanders are trying to steal their belongings.

Right: the death of Captain Cook, based on a sketch by his brother. Cook had gone ashore to retrieve a boat which had been stolen by the Hawaiians. The natives forced him and his men to the water's edge and, when Cook turned to give orders to his men, he was stabbed in the back.

The greatest name in eighteenth-century exploration (and perhaps in the whole history of British exploration) is that of Captain James Cook. In three great voyages he added more to exact geographical knowledge than any other man for centuries. In the first voyage (whose original purpose was to make astronomical observations from Tahiti) he sailed round New Zealand (thus proving it an island) and then crossed the Tasman Sea to discover the east coast of Australia and name that part of the continent where he made his landfall 'New South Wales'. He travelled northwards along it to make his way home across the Indian ocean after passing through the Torres Strait and Timor Sea. This was done between 1768 and 1771. The following year Cook set out again. Sailing from west to east, he was the first man to penetrate the Antarctic circle and to circumnavigate Antarctica. He approached the South Pole more closely than any other eighteenth-century traveller (though it was still 1800 kilometres away). His third and final voyage began in 1776 and lasted until 1779, when it ended, tragically, with his death in the Sandwich islands (Hawaii) at the hands of the native inhabitants. Before that, though, Cook had passed through the Bering Strait in search of a passage from Hudson's Bay to the Pacific and had explored the coasts both of America and of Asia in that region.

Others followed in the tracks of the explorers. British prisons were becoming packed with criminals, who after 1783 could no longer be sent (as had been many for the past century) to the American colonies to get them out of the way. West African convict settlements were tried, but failed. So New South Wales was reconsidered in this light and on 26 January 1788 the first new Australians arrived at Botany Bay, later to be called Sydney – 717 convicts, of whom nearly 200 were women. They made New South Wales a rough, tough place, even when the first free settlers arrived five years later (only eleven of them). But this was the start of the first new European nation established overseas since the North American settlements of the early seventeenth century.

Shortly before 1800 the first Protestant and Catholic missionaries (from Great Britain and France respectively) arrived in Tahiti and the Friendly islands. Christianity made rapid progress in Polynesia. The Pacific was, willy-nilly, at last fully entering the orbit of European civilization. Just after 1800 the naming of a new continent – Australia – by Matthew Flinders (the first man to circumnavigate it) marks the end of one great age of exploration.

The emergence of the USA

The British colonies in North America grew faster than ever in the eighteenth century. A thirteenth, Georgia, was founded in the 1730s by private charity as a way of settling poor emigrants, and this completed their number. Their population went up rapidly, and when George III came to the throne in 1760 he had about two million North American subjects. They were then still increasing at a rate which would double the population every generation and included descendants of many nations besides the English, Irish and Scottish; Dutch families were thickly settled in many areas, Germans in others. And of course there were Red Indians too who were subjects of the English king, and (mainly in the southern colonies) about one sixth of the population were black slaves. Altogether British North America contained about a third as many people as did Great Britain at the same time.

The development of Savannah in Georgia. By 1734, little more than a year after Georgia had been founded, only about half the plots were occupied yet the streets were already being laid out to a grandiose chequer-board plan.

The colonists were spread over a much bigger area than that of the mother-country, and one which had grown a lot since 1700. Broadly speaking, settlers always tended to press inland from the coast until they came to the mountainous barrier running almost the whole length of the eastern coast, of which the Alleghenies are the most important part. Much of this expansion was at the expense of the Indians. It had led to fighting and bad blood on the frontiers of some of the colonies – in particular, those of New York and Pennsylvania, whose settlers showed especial keenness in pressing into the river-valleys which led down from the other side of the mountains to the huge Mississippi basin beyond. At one time in the eighteenth century it looked as if the French pincer-operation of building forts up from New Orleans at the mouth of the Mississippi and down from Canada, would stop any further British-American movement westwards. But in the world-wide Seven Years' War the French lost Canada and that danger disappeared.

Spread over such an area, with many different histories of settlement behind them,

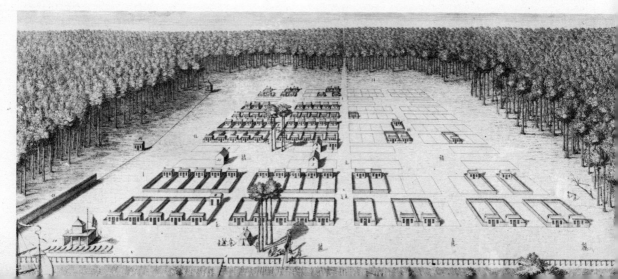

A German colonist, Christopher von Graffenried, founded the colony of New Berne in North Carolina in 1710. On his return to Europe he wrote an account of his journey and illustrated it with his own drawings. Here he and an English surveyor, with their Negro servant, seem to be captives at what he calls 'The Red Indian Tribunal in Catechna'.

different cultural and religious roots and very different economic needs and opportunities, the thirteen colonies were a very varied lot. People sometimes called their inhabitants 'Americans' – but they thought of themselves much more as New Yorkers, or Carolinians or New Englanders. What is more, they were often bitterly antagonistic to one another. Often they quarrelled over their boundaries; sometimes they fought. At times they even fought within one colony – there was a civil war in North Carolina in 1771, for example. All the larger colonies were aware of big differences between the frontiersmen, who lived in the western wilderness, and the townsfolk and planters of the coastal plains (or 'tidewater', as this region was called). There was really very little to hold Americans together and prevent their many divisions from leading to even fiercer quarrels, except that they were all subjects of the English Crown.

In 1763 they thought of themselves as its loyal subjects. Americans were grateful for English protection from the French and Indians during the wars, and the government in London had not made enough demands on them to irritate them. They were different from Englishmen in their attitude to authority, though. They were more easy-going among themselves than the British: the colonies were

new countries and, although they had rich and poor, they had few titled people and nothing like the English tradition of respect for an aristocracy. The differences between the various religious sects were accepted more readily in the colonies than at home: after all, many of the early New England settlers had gone there in the first place to get away from the Church of England, and Maryland had been founded specifically to provide a haven for Roman Catholics.

Though some foreigners had already said that it would prove impossible in the end for England to keep her American colonies, the collapse of the British empire in America – for that was what followed within twenty years of the peace of 1763 – came to most people as a great surprise. There were many causes. The French departure from Canada was one. The colonists thereafter felt they no longer needed the protection of the British so much; some of the more violently Protestant felt irritated by the British tolerance towards the largely Roman Catholic French Canadians. The change in Canada might not have mattered so much had not the British authorities given offence by saying they would not allow further settlement in the west, but would protect the rights of the Indians against settlers by keeping the two peoples apart. Protection of the

Indian turned Americans against the mother country rather as white settlers in Africa were sometimes turned against her in the twentieth century by British protection of black interests. Worse still, to keep Indian and white American apart would need soldiers and that would cost money. As these soldiers would be protecting the white frontiers against Indian raids, it seemed to many people in London only fair that the Americans should pay for them.

For years one government after another tried to find acceptable and workable ways to tax the colonists with this end in view. One

Paul Revere's inflammatory engraving of the Boston 'Massacre' of 1770, the first violent clash between the British and the colonists. Several colonists were killed and given a well-publicized funeral; the soldiers were tried for murder and acquitted.

colonial politician coined the slogan 'no taxation without representation'; if Americans did not send members to the parliament at Westminster, it was argued, why should they pay the taxes it laid down? Gradually discontent grew. People began to feel they might like to remain subjects of King George, but that they would do better if they were not ruled by laws made by parliament, but by laws they

Real fighting between the American colonists and the British began in 1775 at the little village Lexington. In this American engraving, British redcoats are firing on the blue-coated militiamen of Massachusetts.

made themselves. As, in large measure, this was what many of them had really been doing through their own assemblies for years, with very little interference by parliament, the idea easily caught on. But a desire for complete independence from the English Crown was still slow to appear. Even when the first shots of the American Revolution were fired (at a British column on its way to seize some illegal arms held in a little town not far from Boston in 1775), many Americans remained loyal.

By 1776 those who wanted to break with England had grown stronger. A congress of representatives from each of the colonies met that year in Philadelphia and agreed to a Declaration of Independence drawn up by one of the outstanding Americans of his age, Thomas Jefferson. This marked the final parting of the ways. From this moment the only chance the British had of keeping their colonies was to crush the rebellion by force.

A draft of the first few sentences from the American Declaration of Independence. Jefferson's aim, in drafting it, was for it 'to be an expression of the American mind' and 'to place before mankind the common sense of the subject'.

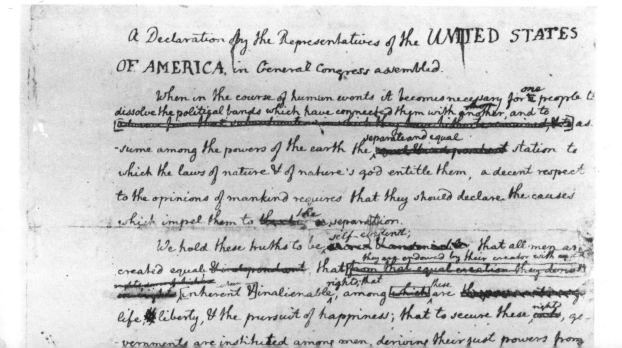

It took seven years for them to admit that they could not do it and withdraw. The issue was decided much earlier, but only in 1783 was peace signed, so that the two groups of Britons could go their separate ways. Fighting and diplomacy had been the deciding factors. In the struggle, though it may not have seemed so on paper at the outset, the odds were by no means all in England's favour. True she had a powerful and well-trained army and navy, and the rebels had none. True, too, that large numbers of Americans were loyal and many stayed so until the end of the war, when thousands went to live in Canada rather than stay in their former homes. Great Britain moreover was rich and her colonies were poor. But against this had to be put other considerations. There was the huge distance which separated the colonies (where the fighting took place) from the home base in Great Britain and the vast problems of transport and supply this led to. Another problem was the terrain, often difficult and badly mapped, hard to live in for European soldiers used to campaigning with good communications and supply depots. Nor could the British fight a really savage campaign – burning farms and so on – which would make it impossible for the colonists' army to survive, because they could not afford to alienate the friends they had. Finally, there were foreigners a-plenty anxious to profit from England's troubles. By the end of the war the British were not only fighting the Americans but the French (who were delighted to have a chance of revenge for the loss of Canada), the Spanish and the Dutch as well. That tipped the naval odds against the British at a crucial moment, forcing the British army to surrender at Yorktown in 1781, the decisive action of the war. That was the real end; fighting dragged on, but after that disaster it was really only a question of when and how the British would come to terms.

So there emerged a new nation: the United States of America, the first decolonialized

George Washington in 1777, when he was commander of the American forces in the war against Britain.

country. The links between the thirteen states (the former colonies) were not very tight, even after they accepted a constitution which brought them together in a federal republic in 1789. But it was clear that some Americans had already grasped that, if the new states were to survive at all, they would have to have some kind of overall government. Among those who thought like this was the former commander of the American army, George Washington, and he now became the first president of the Union.

The two great changes – separation from Great Britain and the creation of even a weak central government for the new 'United States' – were of enormous importance for all mankind, though this was by no means quickly grasped by more than a few. In the first place, the American Revolution can now be seen as the first of a series of colonial revolts which was to unroll for about fifty years and was to take even longer to have its full effects. Indeed, from some points of view, not all of the long-term effects were finally visible until the great decolonizing of the twentieth century. What had been shown long before that, though, was that the era of direct colonial rule over European populations overseas had ended unless that rule was directed towards making the colonies independent. That this was to be the aim of British policy in its 'white' colonies in the next century is largely to be explained by the shock of defeat in America in the eighteenth.

Another result of the American Revolution was that North America was to be opened up, settled and dominated by an independent people who spoke English and shared much of English culture. They took for granted the sort of religious, legal and constitutional tradition which was accepted in England, and spread it across a continent. World history would have been very different if the colonists had been formed, say, by French or Spanish ideas of absolute monarchy. Indeed the founding fathers of the United States pressed some English ideas much farther than they had gone in the mother country. Religious tolerance was taken so far that the government was forbidden by the constitution to support any religion at all. The American republic was thus the first great country to have no church established by law (though religious denominations have always been very important there).

The United States of America was also the first major state to be a republic; the general eighteenth-century view was that republics were feeble and suited only to small states. It was a great thing for mankind when the United States proved this wrong, though it owed much to the young republic's good luck in being remote and rich in natural wealth. The new state was a democracy, too – not perhaps in a perfect sense, but more completely than any other great state. This was a matter of principle: the opening words of the constitution are 'We the People'. Democracy has spread deeper and farther into American life ever since. With it has gone distrust of central government, so that democracy has been accompanied by an unequalled degree of political and practical freedom for American citizens in their everyday lives. There is still no major country of which this is so true.

All these were very important results of the revolution and do much to justify a phrase once used of the republic: 'the world's last, best hope'. They took time to make themselves felt. Immediately the new republic seemed to make very little difference: it was too far away. The British were soon doing more trade with America than before the war, so the political division seemed not to matter all that much. The British might have been snubbed by the French, but the French did not get their colonies back, and had been forced to spend a great deal to support the Americans. The war also made a difference to the way British governments thought about colonies where there were large numbers of settlers. They distrusted them and spent most of the nineteenth century trying to find ways of giving them as much independence as it was safe for them to have as soon as possible so that they would not cost the British taxpayer money or threaten him with a repetition of the American war.

As for the Americans, they were to make haste in consolidating the new republic and enlarging its borders. At the end of the eighteenth century they were still seemingly very weak and divided and it appeared to many European statesmen that not much was to be expected of them.

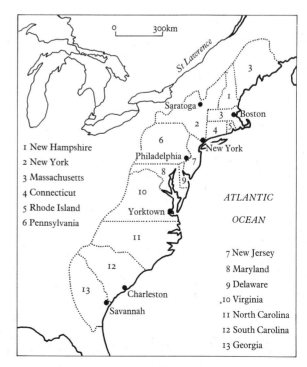

1 New Hampshire
2 New York
3 Massachusetts
4 Connecticut
5 Rhode Island
6 Pennsylvania
7 New Jersey
8 Maryland
9 Delaware
10 Virginia
11 North Carolina
12 South Carolina
13 Georgia

The French Revolution

From the days of Louis XIV until well into the second half of the nineteenth century France was effectively top dog in continental affairs. It is fairly easy to see why. Even after Russia stepped forward as a major power, her huge armies were too far away, her rulers too preoccupied with what was happening to the decaying Turkish empire and with expansion into Asia to be a real force in western Europe all the time. Great Britain might prevail over France in the long colonial duel, but she could never thwart French designs in Europe except with the help of continental allies. The Austrian Habsburgs reigned over a ramshackle empire of semi-independent bits and pieces whose potential strength was almost impossible to mobilize, and they were bogged down in the affairs of Germany or the Holy Roman

Empire, while neither Prussia nor Spain could hope to match the strength of France, which could draw on a population of about twenty-five million at the end of the eighteenth century.

Nonetheless the French state was showing signs of being in grave trouble as the second half of the century rolled on. There was the loss of Canada and the defeat of 1763 at the hands of the British. This was to some extent offset by going to war on the side of the American colonists; the British were defeated and humiliated. But the French did not get Canada back. Moreover they had added hugely to the vast debts of the monarchy; war is a very expensive activity.

One after another, ministers tried to find a way of reducing this debt and giving France

Left: when, in 1789, the deputies of the Estates General who wanted reform and an end to privilege were kept out of their meeting place in Versailles palace, they met at a near-by tennis court. In this painting the deputies are shown swearing not to allow the assembly to be dissolved until it has produced a constitution for the French nation.

Right: a French republic was declared in September 1792, and Louis XVI was tried and executed in the following January.

sensible new financial arrangements. They all failed, basically because they could find no way of making the better-off pay their due share of taxes. It turned out that in some ways the impressive French monarchy was not so powerful after all. It was certainly not so good at raising revenue as the British parliamentary system, for example. More and more the blame for this state of affairs was laid at the door of the French nobility. When, at last, the king announced that in 1789 he would summon the nearest thing to a parliament that France had ever possessed – the medieval 'Estates General' – there was great rejoicing, for times were hard and almost everyone except the nobles hoped that France would at last be governed in accordance with the will of the majority.

In the end that was more or less the outcome, but only after long and bitter political struggles. For when the Estates General met, in May 1789, there began a process by which more and more grievances about many more

things than fair taxation broke out in new demands and more and more people turned to politics to put things right. In the course of this the historic constitution of France was swept away, the absolute monarchy turned first into a constitutional one and then into a republic, the king and queen were executed, thousands of people died in civil war, the old national religion of Roman Catholicism was given up and the Church's property sold for the good of the state, and a thousand and one other changes, big and small, were made. This is what we call the French Revolution. It lasted from 1789 to 1799, when a young general seized power from the politicians and set France again on the road back to monarchy. Nothing like it had ever been seen before.

Nearly all the lasting changes of the revolution were made by the end of 1791. The years from then to 1795 were the most turbulent in its history; after that, things settled down somewhat. France had by then broken defi-

The statue of Louis XIV being demolished in the Place des Victoires, 1792.

nitely with much of her past and had rebuilt her constitution on the basis of equality before the law (nobility had been abolished), religious toleration and the government of France by an elected representative National Assembly which made laws on any matter, without regard to rights or tradition.

A great deal did not change, though. Indeed, life in much of the countryside can hardly have changed at all, and this is not very surprising, given the deeply engrained ways of rural life. The new decimal currency of francs and centimes (still in use today), for example, was not used in country markets for decades; fifty years after 1789, peasants in some places were still counting in the old coins – crowns and sous. Elsewhere the old measurements of league or arpent were still used in preference to the kilometres and hectares brought in by the revolution. Yet in other ways the revolution turned France upside down, and many people never forgave or forgot this.

This was why Frenchmen tended for the next century or so to use the revolution as a touchstone of political opinions. If you were for the revolution, you wanted more people to have the vote; probably wanted a republic; certainly wanted the Church to have less influence than before 1789; and probably believed in free speech and the wickedness of press censorship. If you were against the revolution, you looked for a strong government which would not have to take much notice of elected politicians; you sought to restore the

influence of the Church in the national life at every level; you believed it was wicked to allow harmful opinions to be published and advocated; and you thought that discipline and good order were more important than personal freedom. This was, roughly speaking, the division into 'left' and 'right' which spread into the politics of many other continental countries in the next fifty years. It was invented (and the words began to be used) when conservatives began to sit together to the right of the president in the National Assembly and liberals began to sit together on his left.

The fact that this division spread later to other countries shows the influence of the French Revolution outside France. From the start some of the revolutionaries had said that what they wanted to do in France by way of reform could and should be done in other countries too. They suggested other peoples should follow the same recipe. Later, when the new France found itself (as it did from 1792 for most of the rest of the decade) at war with other nations, they exported revolution by force and propaganda to other countries. French generals set to work to organize revolutions and set up new republics in place of the former governments in lands which they invaded.

This was one reason for a great series of wars which took place between 1792 and 1815. Not only did it seem that France was again setting out on a career of conquest as she had done under Louis XIV, but it looked as if conquest was going now to be followed by revolution. Great Britain was France's most unremitting enemy. Only once and briefly between 1793 and 1814 did Great Britain make peace, and in the end she won the colonial game hands down, once French sea-power had been rendered powerless by the great naval victory of Trafalgar. Fighting on land was a different matter, though. The British long had an expeditionary force serving in Spain, but the huge numbers which eventually defeated France (first in 1799 and then in 1812–13) came from the peasants of Austria, Prussia, and, above all, Russia.

But to leave a picture behind of the French Revolution as merely an aggressive and conquering force would be quite wrong. The French armies often brought liberation with them. The laws they introduced led to the abolition of feudalism and the destruction of old tyrannies, and promoted the equality of men before the law. This was one reason why,

from the outset, the French Revolution was (as it has remained) a great inspiration and ideal. All over the world in the next hundred years men would turn against oppressors real or imaginary in the name of the ideals of the revolution, which can be summed up in one of its own slogans: Liberty, Equality, Fraternity. This is why tyrants feared the revolution. And even when men did not look to revolution as a way of getting what they wanted, they would be inspired by the Declaration of the Rights of Man drawn up by the first National Assembly of France in 1789. It was later redrafted several times, but it gave expression to the idea that men have rights as human beings, not simply because they inherit them from any particular system or law or because they have historical traditions supporting them. This is a noble idea which has inspired men ever since, and it is the main reason why the French Revolution is to be remembered as an event in world history as well as in the history of France.

Map legend:
- French empire 1812
- dependent states
- French allies
- independent countries

SWEDEN

Baltic Sea

RUSSIA

DENMARK Copenhagen

GREAT BRITAIN

PRUSSIA

POLAND

Leipzig

Jena

Waterloo

AUSTRIAN EMPIRE

Paris CONFEDERATION OF THE RHINE

Vienna

FRANCE

ITALY

Marengo

PORTUGAL

Corsica

Rome

NAPLES

SPAIN

Sardinia

Trafalgar

0   500km

The defeat of the French and Spanish fleets at Trafalgar in 1805 convinced Napoleon that an invasion of Britain was impossible. This detail of a painting shows Nelson (who commanded the British fleet) mortally wounded aboard his flagship, the Victory, *towards the end of the battle.*

Napoleon Bonaparte

Besides being an outstanding professional soldier, Napoleon was a master politician and a supreme manager of public relations. He took over any symbol or idea which could strengthen his rule by its associations, from the golden bees which had been the insignia of the ancient Merovingian kings of France to the tricolour of the Revolution of 1789 carried on the 'eagles' (borrowed from the legions of Imperial Rome) borne by his regiments.

Right: the standard of a French regiment from the south-west (the Department of the Landes).

In 1804 Napoleon became 'Emperor of France'. His coronation ceremony was painted by David: Napoleon crowned himself, even though Pope Pius VII had come to Paris for the occasion.

Napoleon appointed Jacques David to capture in paint the dramatic action and pageantry of his regime. One of his commissions was to paint him 'calm on a fiery horse' in this romanticized version of him leading his troops across the Italian Alps. He is presented as a much punier, less dramatic figure by the English cartoonist, Gillray (top right). William Pitt, Prime Minister of Britain, is seated on the left, while Napoleon, on the right, carves the whole of Europe for himself from the 'plum pudding' on the table.

Napoleon was prepared to utilize the latest technical and scientific advances. Below left: In 1801 he invited Volta, the inventor of the pile battery, to Paris to demonstrate his discovery; and his interest in archaeology was commemorated in this plate from the 'Egyptian Service', which shows his scientists measuring the sphinx (which his soldiers also used for gun practice).

New ideas and the Enlightenment

So far this book has been almost entirely about change. We ought to recall the other side of the coin: people's lives changed very little and very slowly in many ways over these centuries. Unless they happened to be involved in an upheaval like the French Revolution, it is not likely that remote villages in central France or southern Germany would have looked very different from how they had looked in the Middle Ages until well into the nineteenth century. Dress, tools, routines, local customs long remained almost unaltered over much of Europe, and in China or India the stagnation must have been even greater.

Obviously, human biology had not changed much; at the end of the eighteenth century, the rich everywhere were likely to be stronger and healthier than the poor, but they were few in number; the great majority of men and women were much more equal in the face of death and more likely to die young than they are today. Even the rich could not draw on much more than better food and nursing to help them resist disease: medicine was not very good. This was not because there had not been important increases in medical knowledge since 1500. Vesalius, the great sixteenth-century anatomist, had opened the way to scientific dissection and observation, which enabled doctors to get away from Galen and Aristotle, and in the next century William Harvey had made the enormously important discovery that the blood circulated (instead of ebbing and flowing as Galen had thought). But this did not make much difference to treatment.

Doctors had a very limited and unscientific repertoire of remedies at their disposal. A Swiss army surgeon called Paracelsus had in the sixteenth century done something to improve diagnosis and introduced specific drugs

Above: an experiment with blood transfusion in the eighteenth century. Doctors had not yet realized that successful blood transfusions could only be made between creatures with the same blood type. (This attempt to give human blood to an animal was doomed to failure.)

Below: a macabre engraving by the English artist Hogarth showing the dissection of an executed criminal – one of a series in which he depicted the brutal side of eighteenth-century life.

which had been chemically prepared. The eighteenth century brought the discovery of the drug digitalis, still used for the treatment of heart disease (and a doctor's best standby for this complaint right down to the twentieth century) as well as the very important technique of inoculation and vaccination. But these had not really had much time to produce an effect before 1800. On the whole, little protection or remedy was available to most patients except their natural immunities and good health.

It was true that some of the ferocious epidemics of the past seemed to abate in Europe as time went by. The attack of plague at Marseilles in 1720 is said to have killed half the population; there was another bad one at Messina in 1743, but this was really the last serious visitation in western Europe. Few people now remember that the English nursery rhyme about 'a ring-o'-roses' was about the seventeenth-century plague. Good quarantine measures, together with more town building in brick and stone (which suits rats less well than houses of wood and wattle) are probably the main explanation for the decline of plague in Europe, but, on the other hand, it was as prevalent as ever in North Africa, Asia and Ottoman Europe. As for typhus and smallpox, these were still recurrent everywhere, while in these three centuries new diseases also appeared where they had not been before. Syphilis had a tremendous effect when

A ward in Guy's Hospital, London. An important step in medicine had come in the eighteenth century with the founding of hospitals as places to treat patients and train doctors; they were vo longer merely hostels for the sick and poor.

it first appeared in Europe at the end of the fifteenth century and when it reached China later, while measles and smallpox devastated the Americas and the Pacific islands when Europeans took them there.

All in all, it can hardly be said that medical science had made much difference to general levels of life-expectancy anywhere in these three hundred years. It had not even done anything to alleviate pain. No anaesthetics existed in 1800 which were any better than the opiates of ancient Greece; a sailor wounded in a sea-battle of the Napoleonic wars would be lucky if he could swallow a mug of rum before undergoing the surgeon's attentions. Aspirins were a century away.

Another thing that did not change much in these centuries, even in Europe, was the position of women. The status and freedom of European women had long been superior to that of women in other civilizations because of the heritage of Christian teaching and practice, which always gave them greater respect than had other religions. European women were not veiled or secluded in the harem; they had in many countries the chance of important public roles if the accident of birth favoured

In eighteenth-century France women held salons or meetings for intellectual conversation. At one such salon given by Madame Geoffrin (third from the right) an actor gives a reading to an audience which includes Rousseau and Diderot.

them – there are no non-European women rulers in this period to compare in power with Isabella of Castile, Elizabeth I of England, Catherine de Medici of France, Queen Anne of England, Maria Theresa of Austria or Catherine the Great of Russia, to cite only the most outstanding of them – and, though law and custom varied much from place to place they could usually own property and often could act in economic affairs with the freedom of men.

Nonetheless they were generally not so favourably placed as men before the law and, of course, they had virtually no access to the professions or higher education unless they had exceptionally enlightened and far-sighted parents who provided them with tuition at home. Queen Elizabeth I, it is worth remembering, liked to debate in Latin with the scholars when she visited her universities and was able to correct the exercises of the students who pronounced orations in that tongue in her honour. In the eighteenth century a number of women, mostly of fairly high social rank, and in France and England more than elsewhere, had begun to make something of a name for themselves in literary and artistic circles, and by 1800 a few women novelists and writers were already well known. These were the tiny beginnings of a new phase of

emancipation for European women, but of course this did not affect any but a few. For this reason some voices began to be raised before the end of the eighteenth century in favour of giving women greater political or legal rights – a more favourable treatment, for example, over the law of marriage. None of this had much effect by 1800. One possible reason was that the French Revolution scared people everywhere about making any changes in the way society was run. And the thought of tampering with something so deeply rooted in popular prejudice as the relations between men and women was especially alarming.

In the end female emancipation would have to wait much longer than the optimists of the eighteenth century hoped, and it would owe more to practical inventions – the factory system, for example, which took women out of the home and into work – than to political and legal change. For most women in the world, in any case, the degree of respect and the status already enjoyed by European women would themselves have been goals beyond their dreams in 1800. Most women then still lived in male-dominated societies, carrying out much of the heavy labour of agriculture, secluded from male society other than that of their own families, worn down by frequent child-bearing (and probably killed by it at an early age too). Even in Europe men were still much more likely then than today to lose at least one wife by her early death and to marry again. This was a very basic inequality indeed, and not one which could be much altered until modern society had revealed its possibilities of creating new wealth.

· At the end of the eighteenth century most Europeans and Americans almost certainly believed that the universe was made by God. But some did not, and many of those who still did held this belief in a way very different from their ancestors of 1500. Then, everyone had believed that the universe was centred on the earth, on which God had placed man, who was His highest creation, with the prospect that, thanks to the Christian religion, man could prepare himself for an eternal life in heaven. By 1800, educated men would have found it much harder to accept all these assumptions without qualification, though a peasant might still have done so. This was a

great change in the history of European society; educated and uneducated people did not merely differ by 1800 in the range and scope of what they knew, but sometimes actually had different basic beliefs.

Another change obvious by 1800 was that dissenting views over religion were more widely tolerated. Hard attitudes had taken a long time to crumble. Even in England, Switzerland and the United Provinces, the most tolerant countries in Europe, there were still restrictions on liberty in 1800; you could not, for example, go to a university in England unless you belonged to the Church of England.

In spite of the conflict which broke out between the Roman Catholic Church and the state during the French Revolution, France's rulers still felt that the French people needed an official religion. In June 1794 a Festival of the Supreme Being was held (below), which was the beginning of an attempt to encourage the adoption of belief in a Supreme Being manifested in Nature.

In France religious toleration had come about only during the revolution. Nevertheless even where the law remained against it, there was a lot more toleration in practice. Europeans had at least stopped burning heretics, and the worst period of persecuting witches was over by 1700.

Another noticeable attitude in some countries towards the end of this period was a new distrust of government and the power of the state. This, again, was perhaps more marked in Great Britain (where parliament had, since the Stuarts, distrusted royal power) and in the young republic of the United States than anywhere else. It also appeared in the repeated attempts to draw up new constitutions for France during the revolution (most of them failed, but they showed what people wanted). This tendency was at the roots of what the nineteenth century would call 'liberalism', which roughly meant distrusting public power and standing up for the rights of the individual.

Both religious toleration and distrust of the powers-that-be carried the implication that men should make up their minds more for themselves. This was one reason why so many European thinkers and writers were so keen on a free press by 1800; they thought it would give people the information they needed to make up their own minds. They believed in education for the same reason. Though such ideas had many (and often very old) roots, they could by no stretch of the imagination have been thought normal in the Middle Ages and old Christian Europe. This is one way in which, when we look back, the Reformation seems so important; it first shattered the unity of belief based on what the Church taught, which had been the main unifying force since Europe took shape in the Dark Ages. Things had moved so fast since Luther's day that even atheistic ideas were advocated by a few writers in the eighteenth century.

They were among the men of the 'Enlightenment'. Broadly speaking, this was based on a faith that the great scientific discoveries of the sixteenth and seventeenth centuries showed both that the universe could be explained and was not at bottom mysterious and that the best instrument for its explanation and exploration was human reason. In particular, the Enlightenment owed a lot to the English philosopher, John Locke, who had shown, it was believed, that Christianity itself could best be defended by reason, and had advocated the free inquiry and toleration which would make it possible to use reason properly for the good of mankind.

It has always been easier to see the importance of the Enlightenment than to describe it. It is too varied to pin down in a phrase. But it made people sceptical and critical of authority. It is in the Enlightenment that we have to seek the origins of the idea that society actually needs people who comment on it and criticize its behaviour, not in the name of tradition but of the right of the human mind to use its reasoning powers. Faith in men's reason and commonsense was central to the Enlightenment. It enabled the leading thinkers of the age to tackle all sorts of problems with a fair hope that they could solve them, given access to accurate information. (This helps to explain why people spoke of the 'Enlightenment' – they believed that allowing light into dark places, so that reason could get to work, was the highest task of men of letters.) Some things in the world about them stood out clearly as evil but the men of the Enlightenment were optimistic reformers; they thought these evils could be removed. Some of them set about trying to do so and often came to distrust religion when they came up against the Church as an obstacle to reform. Yet sometimes they joined hands with Christians. Such an alliance helped to promote one of the most remarkable of all changes in the history of European society, the abolition of slavery. It did not come until after 1800, but the campaign for it had begun well before that.

One of the major events of the Enlightenment was the appearance of a new, twenty-eight-volume encyclopedia, published between 1751 and 1772, which aimed to give an account of all human knowledge. The editor, Diderot, included articles by many famous *philosophes* and scientists, who advocated reason rather than faith as man's guiding principle. The encyclopedia was censored at first, as a threat to religion and government, but by the publication of the last volume much of the official intolerance had been overcome. Some of the main contributors (left) are shown here discussing their ideas at dinner. Voltaire is seated at the back, with his arm raised, and Diderot is on his left. Shown below are some illustrations from the encyclopedia.

Workers complete some of the different stages in making pins. The pin factory was the classic example given by Adam Smith to show the advantages of a division of labour, an idea which would lead to the factory production line.

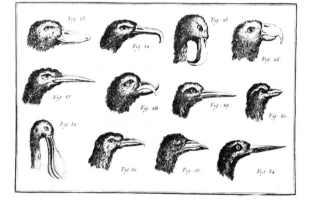

By drawing attention to the shape of the bird's bill the encyclopedia attempted to classify animals as well as showing differences between species.

The fatal thrust demonstrated in an engraving on the art of fencing.

A new economic order

Curiously the most important change in economic thought which took place in these three centuries has been much deplored. This was the growing success of the idea that society is best served if the owner of property has as much freedom as possible to use it to his own profit. Another way of putting this would be to say that society benefits if people seek their own economic benefits by selling their labour, knowledge, skill or resources for the best price they can get. The practical results can be seen in very striking instances – in the abandonment of the old medieval laws against usury, for example, so that people could lend money at interest; or in the dividing up of common land among individuals as private property with which they could do what they liked.

But such contrasts can easily be misleading if exaggerated. Men had been lending money right through the Middle Ages and medieval lawyers were used to arguments that a loan was not really a loan and interest was not really interest. Similarly, medieval landlords had

nothing to learn from anyone about making use of their property rights. Matters have been further confused too by mixing up these changes with another idea, that of the coming of 'capitalism'. It is by no means an easy idea to define, but, if a capitalist is someone who invests savings in a business venture, then there have always been capitalists. What happened from the later Middle Ages onwards was simply that opportunities multiplied enormously and so there were many more capitalists, many of them on a big scale.

Perhaps a better way to describe the change these three hundred years brought to the economics of advanced societies is to say that they led to much more respect than in earlier times for the mechanism of the market. Indeed at times some men almost talked as if it were a divine institution. Men with up-to-date ideas at the end of the eighteenth century were likely to believe that it was almost a scientific law that men's relations with one another were best regulated by their power to buy and sell

The founding of the Bank of England in 1694 – a Dutch idea, partly financed by Dutch capital – did much to give England a sound economic basis in the next century.

Adam Smith, in his Wealth of Nations, *developed many of the ideas of the French economists of the Enlightenment. The book was unique in its systematic and overall presentation of the science of economics and society, and Smith was careful not to push his ideas to extremes, however logical.*

goods and services. Once certain technical matters were defined (what constituted a valid contract, for example, or what was fraud), society should collectively step back, they thought, and let the relations of individuals be decided by market forces.

Such ideas, roughly, were put forward by the greatest thinker about society produced by the eighteenth century, the Scotsman Adam Smith. In his most famous book, *The Wealth of Nations*, published in 1776, he told his readers not to expect their dinners from the benevolence of the butcher or baker, but from the butcher's and baker's sense of their own interest. Broadly speaking, his argument was that, if everyone were free to seek his own profit in commercial transactions – and by 'free' he meant free from the restraints imposed by unfair competition as well as those imposed by the law – then more wealth would be created and so society would benefit.

His book was really an attempt – the greatest that has ever been made – to explain the workings of a free market economy. The ideal 'market society' (as it is sometimes called) which Adam Smith advocated has, in fact, never existed. Pure competition on an equal basis has never been known. Nevertheless, argued Smith and those who followed him, to strive to remove obstacles to individual enterprise, to

'let things go', as one might translate part of a French phrase which became popular about this time (*laissez-faire*), was almost always the best thing to do. This meant, in practical terms, abolishing monopolies or customs dues which kept out competitive foreign products, curbing restrictive practices in guilds of workmen or employers, and so on.

There can be no doubt that Adam Smith identified a number of very fundamental points about the society of his day. No one in the Middle Ages would have said that a man had an absolute right to do what he would with his property if he could make money by it, but ideas were changing in these centuries. Society was moving steadily towards treating all kinds of property, goods and labour simply as commodities – potentially for sale and purchase like anything else in a market which is the best regulator of the distribution of goods we are likely to have. Those who supported such views were convinced that this was the way to greater happiness for more people, to higher standards of civilization and more widely spread wealth.

In a very large measure they were proved right. For all their imperfections, no societies in human history (even very recently) have seen such a rapid increase in their wealth and in the well-being of their members as have done so-called 'capitalist' countries of the last four centuries. Some of this advance was perceptible before 1800, but most of it had then still to come. Much of it must be put down to the opportunities and incentives the market economy created. But some of it arose from another process going on at the same time, which is difficult to disentangle from the acceptance of market ideas, industrialization.

What do we mean by 'industrialization'? One commonsense way of looking at it is to say that it is production organized on a large scale – with many people at work together. But commonsense suggests that we ought to leave agriculture out of this picture, even though it has often employed people in large numbers on the same estate – serfs in eastern Europe, or slaves on plantations, for example – and also trade, which is concerned with exchanging goods, not with making them.

So what do we mean by industrialization when we look at the history of mankind? A rough-and-ready definition would be that it is the process which leads to a society becoming in large measure dependent on manufacturing industry – rather than on trade or agriculture – for its living. And of course, if we look at relatively small areas and not at whole countries, it has been going on for quite a long time. The cloth-making towns of Italy and Flanders in the later Middle Ages, for example, can certainly be said to have been industrialized, providing we keep in mind the fact that they never looked much like what we now think of as an industrial area, with large factories and smoking chimneys. Work in those areas was organized largely on the basis of independent craftsmen with at most a few hands employed by them – boy apprentices and 'journeymen' – who worked in their own houses at looms where they wove wool brought to them by merchants who specialized in this and after-

wards bought their cloth from them. Sometimes such workshops were scattered over a broad area – industry was dispersed throughout the countryside.

The first industries in which something more like the modern large-scale enterprise under one roof or the same management appeared tended to be those handling goods which it was convenient to produce in bulk. An early example was ship-building: ships were getting bigger during these three centuries, and that required more shipwrights at work on the same hull. But they were often still individual craftsmen, taken on for a time to do a specific job and not kept as a permanent paid labour force. Nonetheless state dockyards – those of the republic of Venice, whose fine arsenal can still be seen, or the later royal dockyards at Woolwich and Portsmouth – provide some of our earliest examples of big concentrations of labour and equipment in modern industrial form.

One port which developed rapidly in the eighteenth century was the naval base of Chatham. In the foreground of this picture can be seen its complex of storehouses, shipyards and docks.

Some operations grew steadily in scale as population and rising prosperity increased the demand for products. Brewing was one, and textiles another. Many different things contributed to this. The beginning of the import of cheap cotton from the Americas in the eighteenth century was an enormous encouragement to manufacturers to bring together in one place – and perhaps under one roof – large numbers of workmen who would be kept in employment by the same man. When there was added to this the advantage of having machinery driven by power from an outside source – a water-mill, for example, such as was long used in fulling or paper-making – then the skeleton of the modern factory can be seen.

The interior of a Swedish ironworks in 1781. Up to this date Sweden had led Europe in iron export. However, the Swedish government restricted iron output because they felt that too many forests were being spoilt to provide charcoal for smelting.

By 1800 there were still very few factories in the modern sense, even in England, where the process of concentrating manufacturing had gone farthest. But there were some outstanding and conspicuous examples, which were the pointers to an industrial future. They tended to appear in certain areas. This might be because communications made it easy for them to get the raw materials they needed – there was a great port in Liverpool, for example, which could supply cotton to Lancashire cotton-mills – or because there were

A French ironworks at the end of the eighteenth century. Horses in the background are carrying fuel (usually charcoal) to be fed into the furnace on the right, while water power is used to drive the wheel. In the centre a 'pig' of iron is being weighed.

markets near by, or because there was power available. Power in the early days of industrialization almost always meant muscles, wind or water, and this was still true down to 1800. It was in new machines that the future of manufacturing industry lay. During the eighteenth century the textile industry enormously increased its output per head thanks to inventions which gradually came to widespread use in England (though they had hardly spread beyond it before 1800). The power loom was one of those which especially helped to push work towards the factory and out of the individual workman's cottage or workshop; spin-

ning 'jennies' hugely increased the output of thread. But other industries were not behindhand in turning over more and more of their operations to machines which required tending rather than relying on craftsmen who actually made things themselves. Yet craftsmen were still needed. Behind this development lay the skills slowly accumulated by generations of them – instrument-makers, joiners, smiths, founders, turners and many others. By 1800 we are in sight of the future machine-tool industry, even if it has not yet arrived.

Many of these developments already suggest what were to be some of the most familiar fea-

A replica of a spinning jenny, named after the wife of the inventor, James Hargreave. The first model (1768) could spin only eight threads at once, but it was later developed to handle 120.

The steam pump, used to supply power to the mills and foundries, had been invented in 1712 by Newcomen, yet it was not until 1797 that James Watt perfected this enormous rotative beam engine, regulated by a 'governor', based on Newcomen's design but eliminating most of its disadvantages and able to drive machinery. A key feature of this engine was the governor which kept the steam feed constant in spite of the load.

tures of the modern industrial economy – a flow of mass-produced, cheap goods and therefore new expectations of a higher standard of living; the grouping of a labour force in a large unit under the same roof, where much of the work consists only in tending machines; the growth of a new sort of town, catering for the housing of a large population of workers employed in manufacture; the building of a communications network of ports, canals, roads and eventually railways which makes complex exchanges of materials between different sectors of industry easier and easier. What was not yet obvious – though guessed at by a few outstandingly far-sighted men – was the range of psychological and social impact which such developments might have. That was only to be revealed in the nineteenth century. Then it would be seen that industrialization changed daily life more dramatically than anything since the invention of fire. In three generations Europe was transformed.

One thing which was obvious by 1800 was the lead which Great Britain had already established, and was actually to increase, in the movement towards industrialization. This was partly due to the solidly based agricultural and commercial wealth accumulated there over the previous two centuries. There was also the freedom English society offered to the individual and the large scope to exploit his own talents: European countries where rank, tradition and privilege counted for much more suited enterprising men less well. Even geographical position helped, in that the age of the great discoveries had suddenly made the British Isles the centre of a new network of Atlantic communications, instead of a fringe country at the edge of a world looking towards the Mediterranean. Finally, there were England's natural resources – coal and iron. These were to be exploited in the next century when England's citizens proudly claimed her the title of 'Workshop of the World'.

The world of 1800

By 1800 the inhabited world had become a true unity for the first time in history, and this was brought about by the Europeans, whose civilization had changed more than any other since 1500. At the most basic level it was richer and had begun to offer greater chances of life and well-being to many of those who lived within it. A French peasant's child at the end of the eighteenth century might still have only the life-expectation at birth of an Indian peasant's, but many other European children could already look forward to a far better prospect of survival than that. There was, quite simply, more to eat than three hundred years earlier, and the increase of European population had broken free of the wave pattern of earlier times, even if this could not be understood by the people who were living then.

There could also be seen the beginnings of a European political domination. True, the bulk of the British colonies had broken away to form the United States. The Spanish and Portuguese American empires too, though this could not be known in 1800, were within a few decades of winning independence. But direct colonial rule is not the whole story of Europe's world supremacy and never was to be. The new Americans were still for a long time Europeans in America; they could not shake off their origins, however much they might have to adapt European civilization to the New World conditions. And, in any case, plenty of direct colonial rule remained, most of it British.

Other forms of European predominance already existed. Some were economic. Europeans might be kept out of the trade of some areas by local rulers, or restricted to narrow zones in some countries, but both formally and informally they traded the world round. After the seventeenth century European commercial enterprise never slackened. Slowly it bound the globe more and more tightly together in an economic unity.

Other influences also spread outwards from Europe. One of the first and most striking results of the age of discovery and expansion was the geographical spread of Christianity. Names on modern maps still reflect it. When Vasco da Gama rounded Africa in 1497, he sailed north and on his way touched the coast on 25 December. And so Natal got its name, from the Portuguese for 'Christmas'. The island of Madagascar was first known as St Lawrence, and the major Mexican port of the Gulf, where Cortés landed, is still called Vera Cruz – the 'true cross'. Sacramento, Santa Fé and Providence are other well-known American place-names based on Christian terminology, and hundreds of others can be found the world round. Christianity had its first great age of expansion since the conversion of eastern Europe and Russia in the Middle Ages, thanks to European overseas enterprise. In the Americas whole populations were to become Christians, at least in a formal sense; in the Spanish and Portuguese possessions this happened by conversion of the natives, and in the British and French colonies of the north by immigration and natural increase. In Asia the story was different: no large Christian population appeared very quickly there, except briefly in Japan, where it was wiped out early in the seventeenth century.

Non-Europeans were for a long time not much impressed by differences between the various shades of white person they encountered. All Europeans tended at first to look much alike to them. As far away as China they were called by the name used by Byzantines and Arabs centuries before: 'Franks' (though somewhat mispronounced). In much the

*European family life in the eight-
eenth century – two views : while
in some respects the life of poorer
families had changed very little
for centuries, the middle and
upper classes had much benefited
from the industrial, agricultural
and commercial developments of
those years.*

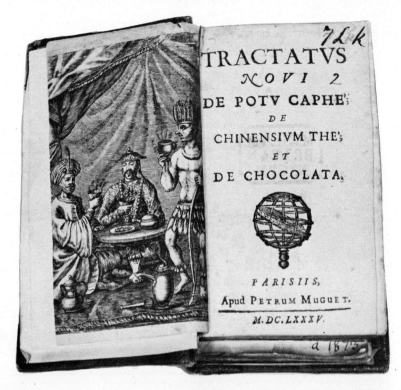

The frontispiece from a French seventeenth-century tract on the new drinks brought to Europe, mainly by the East and West Indian trade. Coffee, chocolate and tea houses became extremely popular and served as meeting grounds for business and literary people and to some extent supplemented the smart salons where new ideas were discussed and exchanged by educated people.

same way many Europeans failed to make distinctions between the peoples with whom they came into increasing contact. This was in some ways a backward step – as early amazement at the wonders of Moghul Delhi, or the shah's capital at Isfahan, or admiration for the seeming tolerance and wisdom of the Chinese crumbled on closer acquaintance, they were replaced by a growing European arrogance and feeling of superiority. This, more marked in the following century, is easy enough to understand even by 1800. A growing concern with progress in Europe, self-congratulation over increasing wealth, humanitarian ideas from the Enlightenment and the confidence still surviving that Christian culture must be the best in the world, all contributed to it. Still more did a feeling of growing political and military power.

It was in this area that some of the most startling changes of these three hundred years had come about. The armies which fought the wars of the French Revolution were numbered in hundreds of thousands; in comparison those of the sixteenth century had been puny. Similarly one broadside from a French or British line-of-battle ship of 1799 could have blown Drake's *Golden Hind* to pieces without more ado. This growth of military power changed the relationship of European armed strength to that of other civilizations. When the British government decided in the middle of the eighteenth century that it must for the first time send regular soldiers to India and not leave it to the Company's native troops to stick up for British interests there, they sent only one battalion – about six hundred men – but it was enough because the training and discipline of European soldiers were so much superior to that of any of the native armies they might encounter.

Such changes are part of the process by which the diplomatic world of 1500 was changed by 1800 into one where what really mattered most was the relatively small group of European 'great powers' (though that term had not then been invented). Some of them had world-wide interests; no non-European power had. The great Asian states played almost no part in affairs outside their immediate sphere. China and Japan were still too remote and un-opened, Moghul India had collapsed and Ottoman power was crumbling. All the great powers whose relations were to shape the his-tory of the next century were European or (in the case of the United States) European in origin. Two of them, Great Britain and Russia, were true world powers. Russia's great eighteenth-century expansion at the expense of Poland and the Turks has distracted attention from her steady pressure in Asia. The business of settling her frontiers there had already brought her into conflict with China and the Persian empire. As for Great Britain, her totally different empire, based on commerce and sea-power rather than military strength, was world-wide even after the loss of the American colonies. But one of these two new world-powers was in some ways the most advanced of European states and the other was the most backward.

It would still take a long time for the full meaning of Europe's onslaught on the world – well under way by 1800 – to appear. Yet what might well have been spotted at even so early a date was that its consequences for the rest of the world would be very mixed. Unquestion-ably Europeans often brought higher civi-lization with them. But they also brought disruptions to old ways, the blind impact of new economic forces and the undermining of old authorities. These all have to be taken into account, together with the more obvious and horrific effects of slaving, or the introduction of alcohol and firearms to backward peoples, or the unconscious spreading of disease. Like most historical balance-sheets, this is a very difficult one to draw up.

The 'Tobacco Parliament' of Frederick I of Prussia – an informal meeting of the king and his advisers, where they would discuss matters of state over a pipe.

In England during the eighteenth century the House of Commons with its elected members and formal debating became established as the centre of political power.

Time chart

1494 Treaty of Tordesillas between Spain and Portugal dividing new worlds to be discovered
1498 Vasco da Gama sails round Cape to India
1501 Safavids begin to rule in Persia (to 1722)
1502 First black slaves arrive America
1507 Mozambique settled by Portuguese
1510 Portuguese occupy Goa (first India territory governed by Europeans since Alexander the Great)
1513 Balboa crosses isthmus of Panama. Pacific sighted
1514 Persians and Ottomans at war
1516 Erasmus publishes annotated Greek New Testament
1517 Martin Luther publishes his 96 'theses' at Wittenberg; Protestant Reformation begins
1520 Magellan crosses Pacific from S. America to Philippines, then dies. Suleiman the Magnificent, Sultan (to 1566), rules from Baghdad to Hungary
1521 First voyage round the world completed by Magellan's crew under Del Cano. Anabaptist movement founded at Wittenberg
1526 Ottomans defeat Magyar army, Mohacs Field, Hungary
1525-7 Babur invades India, founds Moghul Empire which flourishes until death of Aurangzeb (1707), then decline until 1857 and banishment of Bahadur Shah. Empire reaches greatest extent second half seventeenth century
1529 First Ottoman siege of Vienna
1530 Henry VIII begins his quarrel with the Papacy
1531 Pizarro destroys Inca regime, Peru
1532 Anabaptists seize Münster (until 1535). John Calvin begins Reformation movement in Paris
1534 Henry declared by Parliament Supreme Head of Church in England. He is excommunicated by Pope Clement VII, 1533
1540 Jesuits sanctioned by Pope; Ignatius Loyola founder
1542 Portuguese traders arrive in Japan with firearms
1543 Copernicus publishes *De revolutionibus orbium coelestium*
1545 Council of Trent, N. Italy (it sat, on and off, until 1563) assembles to put the Church in order
1548 Peace of Augsburg – Germany divides into Catholic and Protestant
1549 Jesuit, St Francis Xavier, brings Christianity to Japan. First Jesuit missions, S. America
1550s Period of religious wars, Europe, until 1648. Russian colonization of the steppe begins: capture and annexation of Khanate of Kazan (1552); of Astrakhan (1556); conquest of Siberia (1581-1639). United Provinces come into existence led by Holland
1553 British discover northern maritime route to Russia
1557 Portuguese set up first permanent European settlement in China, at Macao
1559 First papal 'Index' of prohibited books
1570 Novgorod razed by orders of Ivan IV, massacre of inhabitants. Nagasaki opened to foreign trade
1584 Sir Walter Raleigh's expedition to Virginia
1585 Japan: Hideyoshi rules all Japan, except for Kyushu and the Kwanto. His leadership brings Japan under central control; he orders Christians expelled (1587) and invades Korea (1592)
1598 Matteo Ricci (Jesuit) at Peking. Edict of Nantes issued by Henry IV of France gives rights to French Protestants (revoked 1685 by Louis XIV)

1600 East India Company founded in London. In Japan Tokugawa Ieyasu is appointed *shogun* (1603); beginning of Tokugawa era with capital at Edo (Tokyo), lasts to 1867. Self-imposed isolation. Between 1622 and 1638 persucution of Christians reaches its peak. Except for Dutch, Europeans expelled and prohibited entry from 1638
1605 Gunpowder plot – conspiracy to blow up James I and English Parliament discovered and blamed on Catholics
1607 First British settlement, Jamestown, N. America
1608 Champlain builds fort at Quebec
1609 Independence of United Provinces recognized by Spain
1612 East India Company establishes first trading station Surat, India
1613 Galileo's dissertation on solar spots advocates Copernican system, provokes his censure by the Church. Russia: Romanov dynasty founded by Michael, tsar 1613-45
1616 Copernicus' doctrines officially banned by Catholic Church. Galileo ordered to abstain in future from condemned doctrines
1618 Protestant Bohemians revolt against Catholic Ferdinand; Thirty Years' War begins. Ends with Peace at Westphalia, 1648. Brandenburg and Prussia united
1620 *Mayflower* expedition. 'Pilgrims' land and found colony at Plymouth, Mass.
1628 William Harvey publishes his treatise on circulation of the blood
1632 Galileo publishes *A Dialogue on the Two Chief Systems of the World*. 1633 He is condemned by Inquisition
1637 René Descartes' *Discourse on Method*
1639 English found Fort St George, Madras
1642 England's Parliament presents 19 Propositions which would transfer sovereignty from king to parliament. Charles I rejects them and civil war erupts (to 1645 with Cromwell's victory at Battle of Naseby)
1643 Evangelista Torricelli, Italian physicist, invents barometer
1644 China: end of Ming Dynasty. Manchu Ch'ing Dynasty begins (to 1912)
1648 England's second Civil War begins with Scots, now allies of Charles I. He is beheaded as a 'tyrant, traitor, murderer and public enemy', 1649. Beginning of the Commonwealth
1649 Ireland: Cromwell captures Drogheda and Wexford
1652 English and Dutch begin first of three Anglo–Dutch wars for overseas commerce (to 1654). Ireland: land confiscation begins
1653 Cromwell made Lord Protector of the English Commonwealth, Long Parliament dissolved
1654 Russia: wars with Poland over Ukraine (to 1657)
1655 English capture Jamaica from Spaniards
1664 France founds her East India Company
1665 Great Plague of London
1666 Colbert founds French Academy of Sciences
1650-1701 Period of wars in Europe: Dutch with English; Dutch with French; English with French; Habsburgs with France. Great Northern War between Sweden and alliance of Poland, Denmark and Russia (Russian defeat at Swedish hands, Battle of Narva, 1700)

1674 Nieuw Amsterdam becomes British by treaty, re-named New York

1676 Russia: war with Ottoman Empire (to 1681)

1682 Louis XIV moves to new Palace of Versailles

1683 Turks invade Habsburg lands in E. Europe. Vienna besieged again by Ottomans. Highwater mark of Ottoman power

1687 Turks evacuate Hungary. Newton publishes *Philosophiae Naturalis Principia Mathematica* in which he announces the law of universal gravitation

1688 The 'Glorious Revolution'. Flight of James II, last of Stuart kings. William and Mary begin their reign. Japan: Genroku Era until 1704 – new urban culture, flourishing of romantic novel, *haiku* poetry and *kabuki* drama.

1689 John Locke's *Letters on Toleration* published defending religious liberty

1690 Ireland's Battle of the Boyne, William III victor

1694 Bank of England founded to lend money to the government. The French Academy issues first edition of its dictionary

1695 Ireland: beginning of penal laws against Catholics

1696 Peter the Great takes Azov from the Turks

1701 Louis XIV against Grand Alliance (England, Holland and Austria). War of the Spanish Succession begins. Peace of Utrecht ends war 1713

1709 Russia: construction of St Petersburg begins (Russian capital transferred there 1712)

1711 Sir Christopher Wren's St Paul's Cathedral officially completed

1720 Japan: ban lifted on foreign books providing they are not Christian. Ireland: Act declares British parliament's right to legislate for Ireland

1736-9 Turkey at war with Austria and Russia

1739 War of Jenkins' Ear between England and Spain. Under Nadir Shah, Persians sack Delhi, take Peacock Throne and Koh-i-Noor from Moghuls

1740 War of Austrian Succession (ends with peace officially declared Aix-la-Chapelle, 1748)

1756 War between France and England, Prussia and Austria (Seven Years' War), peace in 1763

1756-7 India: Battle of Plassey; British domination of Bengal, Calcutta taken

1758 Aoki Konyo introduces sweet potato to Japan; publishes first Dutch/Japanese dictionary

1759 Canada: Wolfe defeats Montcalm outside Quebec; both generals killed

1763 Peace of Paris between Britain, France, Spain and Portugal; Canada ceded to Britain. Peace of Hubertsburg between Prussia and Austria

1765 Stamp Act passed by British Parliament. Stamp Act Congress meets at New York; adopts Declaration of Rights and Liberties

1766 Stamp Act repealed: Declaratory Act asserts right of British Parliament to make laws for British colonists

1768-71 Captain James Cook explores east coast of Australia, names it New South Wales

1769 James Watt's first steam engine

1770 Boston 'massacre'

1772 First Partition of Poland (second Partition 1793, third Partition 1795). By 1800, Russia dominant power in E. Europe

1772-1885 British 'Raj' extends over most of India

1773 Boston 'Tea Party'

1774 Quebec Act closes Ohio country to seaboard settlers. First Continental Congress meets Philadelphia; Declaration of Rights and Grievances drawn up. Russia

gains overlordship of Crimean Tartars. By 1800 Ottoman Empire in decline (though the dynasty survives to 1923-4). Turks accept Russian-dictated Treaty of Kutchuk Kainardji

1775 Skirmishes at Lexington and Concord; War of American Independence begins (1783, with British recognition of independence of USA). George Washington first president

1776 Adam Smith, *The Wealth of Nations*. *Declaration of Independence* drawn up by Jefferson at Philadelphia

1787-91 Russia: war with Ottoman Empire

1788 First Federal Congress of the US at New York

1789 Beginning of French Revolution, storming of the Bastille. *Declaration of the Rights of Man and the Citizen*. Republic proclaimed 1792. Louis XVI beheaded (1793)

1791-2 US and Russia try to open up trade with Japan

1792-9 French Revolutionary Wars: Britain at war with France to 1802 (Peace of Amiens).

1793 British mission, headed by Lord Macartney, arrives China

1798 Thomas Malthus publishes *Essay on Population*

1801 Union of Great Britain and Ireland – United Kingdom. First Census, Great Britain

Acknowledgements

The author and publishers would like to thank the following for their kind permission to reproduce illustrative material:

Aldus Archives for p. 92; J. Allan Cash for p. 11 *left*; George Allen & Unwin for pp. 8–9; Amsterdam Historical Museum for p. 33; Bank of England for p. 112; Biblioteca Ambrosiana for p. 41 *bottom right*; Biblioteca Reale di Torino for p. 65 *above*; Bibliothèque Nationale, Paris/Martine Klotz for p. 101; British Museum for pp. 7 *above*, 15 *right*, 34 *below*, 37 *right*, 42 *left*, 43 *right*, 46, 51 *below*, 51 *above*, 54 *left*, 62, 71 *right*, 87, 91 *above*, 106 *below*, 116 *above*; Photographie Bulloz for pp. 102, 105 *below left*, 109; Connecticut Historical Society for p. 97 *above*; Douglas Dickins F.R.P.S. for pp. 77 *left*, 77 *right*, 81 *below*, 81 *above*, 89 *above*; Werner Forman Archive for pp. 2 *left*, 67 *left*, 89 *below*; Germanisches Nationalmuseum, Nürnberg for pp. 26 *below*, 38; Giraudon for p. 108; Sonia Halliday for pp. 76 *left*, 76 *right*; Robert Harding for p. 18 *left*; Robert Harding/Freer Gallery for p. 80 *above*; Robert Harding/Lutherhalle, Wittenberg for p. 24; Robert Harding/The Earl of Elgin and Kincardine/National Gallery of Scotland for p. 19; Andre Held/Lausanne Museum for p. 28; p. 30 reproduced by Gracious Permission of Her Majesty the Queen; Michael Holford for pp. 3 *left*, 3 *right*, 32 *above*, 49 *left*, 60, 80 *below*, 88, 93, 105 *below right*, 119 *above*; Library of Congress for p. 97 *below*; p. 31 by Permission of the Master and Fellows, Magdalene College, Cambridge; Mansell Collection for pp. 18 *right*, 18 *centre*, 23 *below*, 26 *left*, 39 *above*, 84, 105 *above right*, 111 *above left*, 111 *below right*, 113; Metropolitan Museum of Art for p. 96; Metropolitan Museum of Art (Rogers Fund) for p. 14; Musées Nationaux, Paris for pp. 32 *below*, 53, 100, 104 *above*, 104 *below*, 105 *above left*; National Army Museum for p. 68; National Gallery for p. 21; National Library, Switzerland for p. 95; National Maritime Museum (Crown Copyright reserved) for pp. 47, 103 *below*; National Maritime Museum for p. 114; National Maritime Museum/Michael Holford for p. 7 *below*, 48; Nationalmuseum, Sweden for p. 115; National Portrait Gallery for pp. 35, 121 *right*; New York Public Library for p. 94; Pennsylvania Academy of Fine Arts for p. 98; Photomas for pp. 15 *left*, 45 *below*, 49 *right*; Photoresources (C. M. Dixon) for pp. 10 *left*, 10 *right*, 11 *right*, 72 *left*, 73; Radio Times Hulton Picture Library for p. 45 *left*; Gerhard Reinhold, Leipzig-Mölkau for p. 25; Rijksmuseum, Amsterdam for p. 57; Royal Library, Windsor Castle for p. 41 *below centre*; Royal Picture Gallery, Hague for p. 44; SCALA for pp. 36, 40, 41 *above left*, 41 *above right*, 41 *below left*; Science Museum for pp. 116 *below*, 117 *above*; Victoria and Albert Museum for p. 66 *above*; Wellcome Museum for pp. 106 *above*, 107.

The maps on the following pages are by Kathleen King: 12, 17, 29, 50, 56, 59 *right*, 65 *below*, 69, 71 *left*, 75 *right*, 79, 83 *right*, 99, 103 *left*.

Index